Appillionaires: Secrets from Developers Who Struck It Rich on the App Store

Appillionaires: Secrets from Developers Who Struck It Rich on the App Store

Chris Stevens

A John Wiley and Sons, Ltd, Publication

A catalogue record for this book is available from the British Library.
Set in 9.5 Minion Pro by Andrea Hornberger
Printed in the U.S. by Courier

To Miles Harry Teather. Explore the world with all your heart.

PUBLISHER'S ACKNOWLEDGEMENTS

Some of the people who helped bring this book to market include the following:

Editorial and Production
VP Consumer and Technology Publishing Director: Michelle Leete
Associate Director–Book Content Management: Martin Tribe
Associate Publisher: Chris Webb
Publishing Assistant: Ellie Scott
Development Editor: Kezia Endsley
Copy Editor: Kezia Endsley
Editorial Manager: Jodi Jensen
Senior Project Editor: Sara Shlaer
Editorial Assistant: Leslie Saxman

Marketing
Senior Marketing Manager: Louise Breinholt
Marketing Executive: Kate Parrett

Composition Services
Compositor: Melanee Habig
Proofreader: Susan Hobbs
Indexer: Steve Rath

About the Author

Chris Stevens is the designer behind multiple number-one apps, most famously *Alice for the iPad*. *Alice* is installed on half a million iPads worldwide and counting. Gizmodo called it "The cleverest iPad book yet" and the BBC said it was "A glimpse of the future of digital reading". *Alice for the iPad* was also a guest on *The Oprah Winfrey Show*, where Oprah told her audience it would "change the way kids learn." His other hit app includes *Alice in New York*. Chris also collaborated on the number-one app *Nursery Rhymes with Storytime*.

Chris was a formerly a technology columnist for *The Daily Telegraph* newspaper, and later wrote for *The Times*. He also presented and directed *Space Bubble*, the popular CNET gadget show. Alongside his writing, Chris is an illustrator and scriptwriter. He has worked for Warner Bros, EMAP, and *Wired*. Chris won a Guardian Media Award for his work as a journalist, and famously discovered reflectoporn.

Today Chris runs Atomic Antelope, the publishing house that created *Alice for the iPad*. He spends his time working on book and game titles for the iPhone and iPad, writing, and acting.

Acknowledgments

Thank you to Mills for his encouragement, support, and extraordinary help in tracking down the Appillionaires whose stories are included in this book. Thank you to the wonderful Susan Sunde for pointing me in the right direction and reading stories out loud. Thank you to Bob Logan and Natalie Logan for conversation and adventure. Thank you to Rishi Anand, Andrew Lim, and Hunter S. Thompson. Thank you also to Kezia Endsley, Chris Webb, Ellie Scott, Katherine Parrett, and the brilliant team at Wiley whose commitment to excellence, patience, and kindness is unmatched. Finally, thank you to Steve Jobs and Apple Inc. for making the Appillionaire phenomenon possible.

Appillionaire |ˌAppiləˈne(ə)r; ˈAppiləˌner|

noun

a person whose app has made more than one million dollars on the App Store. Or a person who has generated significant personal wealth by selling apps.

ORIGIN early 19th cent.: from French *millionaire*, from *million*.

Contents

PART II: THE APPILLIONAIRES 59

THE BIRTH OF THE APP

1

INTRODUCTION

THEY ARE THE *Appillionaires:* Smart, ambitious dreamers in bedrooms and garages across the world, plotting the future of mobile apps. Their tools are inexpensive — a MacBook Pro and an iPhone — but overnight the Appillionaires can amass a fortune from selling software on the iTunes App Store. They lead a revival of the hobbyist programmer. Not since the days of the Commodore 64 and Atari 2600 has indie software been sold by such tiny teams of programmers to such massive numbers of consumers.

The money flows to the Appillionaires even as they sleep. While they dream their *Angry Bird*-dreams, invisible electronic transfers push money into the Appillionaires' bank accounts from App Stores in over 80 different countries. As much as $250 million gets spent at the App Store in a single month. Over 10 billion apps have been sold on the store to date and it's estimated that Apple has signed up at least 79,000 software publishers to the iOS (iPhone and iPad operating system) club.

What's remarkable is that Apple's credibility was bolstered so much by the success of the iPod and iPhone that the rise of the iPhone app was widely predicted. Even before the launch of the App Store back in 2008, *Wired* magazine speculated, "iPhone software development may spark a software gold rush not seen since the heyday of PC-platform development in the 1990s."

THERE'S GOLD IN THEM HILLS

It's this label "gold rush" that has been most often applied to the App Store. The potential for success, and risk of failure, is so great that in many ways the App Store has provoked a gold rush among developers. Although the successes are spectacular, the failures are apocalyptic. The mainstream press focuses on the glorious few and gives very little attention to the money being lost on the App Store — a problem compounded by the embarrassed silence of those struggling to turn a profit on their work. In a climate where approximately 540 apps are submitted for review every day, it's easy to see why the Appillionaires are an exclusive and rare breed.

Back in the 80s a catastrophic failure to sell software was a more obvious and public humiliation. Take Atari's *E.T. the Extra-Terrestrial (1982)*, a failed videogame which left the company with losses of over $100 million and the embarrassing problem of what to do with 3.5 million unsold *E.T.* cartridges (the answer, apparently, was to bury them in a New Mexico landfill). But today such failures are even harder to see with the naked eye. For every Appillionaire, there are several thousand invisible, failed app developers. These developers have had their dreams of app superstardom cruelly smashed into a million little pixels. More humbling still is the realization that, despite everything the App Store has done to democratize software development, ultimately success may come from more unpredictable forces than basic hard work. Most indie developers struggle to get any attention for their apps — they simply don't have the marketing clout of giant corporations and must rely entirely on their placement in the App Store. For many, the only real chance of success is to be featured by Apple in one of the highly desirable iTunes banner adverts.

> As iPhone developer Sean Maher points out, "you can't put 'get featured by Apple' in your business plan any more than you can put 'win the lottery' in your personal budget."

The Appillionaires are engaged in trench warfare against each other, and against the traditional publishers of corporate America's vanguard. App development has become a cut-throat industry where an increasing small number of independent players battle it out for the attention of over 180 million iPhone and iPad owners, each of these owners downloading around five apps per month. The competition is so intense that the App Store is scarred by the Appillionaire's rivalry. Shills have been known to clog up their rival's apps with bad reviews on iTunes, while writing positive reviews for their own apps. Apple's Phil Schiller has gone as far as to remove a developer called Molinker from the App Store for cheating the reviews system by positively rating its own apps. The end result was that Molinker had all of its 1,100 apps pulled from the store and was shamed globally by thousands of blogs. Some developers have discovered shill reviews on their apps, traced these back to rival companies, and phoned the CEO to ask why his head of mobile marketing was writing reviews of competing apps.

Tensions between competitors are inevitable because the Appillionaires fight it out in a crowded landscape of over 160,000 apps. It's a place where millions of dollars can be made or lost in an instant; where dropping off the top-ten in the App Store means an exponential decline in sales, obscurity, and even ruin. It's a bizarre, upside-down chaos where venture capitalists might spend millions on an app, only to discover themselves beaten to the top spot in the App Store by a 15 year old armed with nothing more than a Mac and a dog-eared copy of *Objective-C For Dummies*. The size of your corporation and the scale of your investment can be outmatched simply by the intellectual prowess of your competitor working out of his or her bedroom.

APP STORE ROULETTE

Given its unpredictability, what makes the App Store so popular? One theory is that we enjoy the strange psychological lure of uncertainty. Researchers have discovered that we often find relationships more compelling if the object of our affection is mysterious and non-committal. The image of a girl sat on a lawn picking petals from a flower and musing, "He loves me, he loves me not" is a fairly accurate depiction of a developer's relationship with Apple. On one hand the girl with the flower hopes that "he" loves her, but on the other hand a lot of the fun is down to not knowing. It's human nature that we are attracted to the thrill of never being quite sure where fortune will smile, and there are few businesses where that feeling is more acute than iOS development. Everything about the process is uncertain.

Developer Daniel Markham calls iPhone development "App Store Roulette," and Andy Finnell of the software studio Fortunate Bear cautions against hoping for App Store success, "you're betting a lot of this on luck, and the odds are stacked against you. You'd have better odds playing slots at a casino."

Indeed, as much as app development has been called a gold rush, there is an equally loud theory that it operates more like a casino.

"The closest thing I've seen to a 'business model' for marketing iPhone apps is to advertise like crazy until you get into the top 50," says David Barnard of AppCubby, "once you're there, the top 50 list will start generating its own buzz… But that's not a business model, that's like rolling the dice at a casino."

The counter-argument is that life itself is hard, very much like rolling a dice at times. It might be that the App Store simply gives developers the illusion of an ordered system, with top-ten lists and sales tracking, but ultimately it is human nature and the unpredictable whim of the masses that determine the success of an app. The App Store might look like an ordered system, but really it's just a layer over the messy reality of selling anything.

CHALLENGES WITH THE APP STORE

The App Store does present some unusual problems though. For one: the sheer number of apps available. Craig Hockenberry, who made the popular iPhone app *Twitterific*, complained as early as 2008 that a race to the bottom on prices meant his team could not invest time and money in great apps. "We have a lot of great ideas for iPhone applications," said Hockenberry, "Unfortunately, we're not working on the cooler (and more complex) ideas. Instead, we're working on 99¢ titles that have a limited lifespan and broad appeal. Market conditions make ringtone apps most appealing."

But in the intervening years, the 99¢ price has not won out completely. App developers 2D Boy sold more than 125,000 copies of *World of Goo* for the iPad priced at $4.99 in just two months and several best-selling iPad book apps have also skirted $9 or more. Developers sometimes attempt to make money simply by selling enough apps at the cheapest possible price, but this isn't always the best plan. Often a lower price just invites a torrent of abusive reviews from younger, more flippant users who take a chance on an app they don't really want. Still, deciding what to charge for an app remains a strange art, and only adds to the curious reverence many of us feel towards the Appillionaires.

The App Store is also unusual and unpredictable because it's a hugely significant distribution method for the creative arts, but it's controlled by a single all-powerful god: Apple Inc. The company decides what is and isn't allowed to be sold in the App Store. Although critics like those who work for *The New York Times* initially warned that Apple's censorship of apps would "discourage [developers] from spending nights and weekends working on new and useful applications," in the end it seems to have had little effect other than to reassure consumers and generate even more publicity for the iPhone and iPad.

World of Goo in action. This deliciously addictive physics puzzler has sold millions of copies.

SOURCE: Copyright 2D Boy Ltd.

Since the opening of the App Store there have been a litany of complaints and high-profile criticism of Apple's policies. These reached a crescendo when Trent Reznor of the band Nine Inch Nails reacted to a rejection notice from Apple on the grounds that his app "contains objectionable content." In reply Reznor wrote, "Thanks Apple for the clear description of the problem - as in, what do you want us to change to get past your stupid standards?"

Apple accepted the app a few days later, refusing to comment on what had changed its mind.

THE APP COMMUNITY

In the midst of all this confusion and competition, there are also stories of great friendship and, often, a wonderful sense of camaraderie among the Appillionaires. The community of people behind the apps you use on your iPhone and iPad are uniquely creative and communicative, often building extremely close friendships with other app makers. Take characters like Mills from ustwo, the self-styled "King of Failure," and a Twitter superstar who takes as much pride in his app disasters as his successes. Mills is the closest thing the industry has to a cultural barometer, providing a constant stream of consciousness direct from the mind of a leading app developer. To read his Twitter feed is to witness first-hand the turmoil in the soul of an Appillionaire. As his company's apps drift wildly in and out of the top ten, his tweets tread a spectrum of emotion, from the heartwarming advice, "make love… not code," to, later in the day, simply, "I give up."

Nursery Rhymes with Storytime is Mill's most successful indie app to date.

SOURCE: Copyright ustwo Ltd and Atomic Antelope Ltd.

This book is also going to introduce you to the smaller teams, like Johnny Two Shoes: Two brothers, Max and Scott Slade, who created the indie pirate romp, *Plunderland*, an app that allowed them to drop out of the nine-to-five slog and embark on a philosophical adventure, punctuated by late-night coding binges. "I just get to do what I want to do now," says Max, who made over $16,000 a day at the height of *Plunderland's* success.

The smash hit pirate-themed caper, *Plunderland,* created by Max and Scott Slade.
SOURCE: Copyright Johnny Two Shoes Ltd.

With an appetite for glory coupled with 24-hour access to the Internet, relationships are strong in this industry. The Appillionaires are sometimes friends and often relatives. They may even be husband and wife, like the team behind *Harbor Master,* who you'll revisit later in this book. They eschew all traditional visions of the storefront; Appillionaires work from garages, bedrooms, and cafés, and then distribute their creations electronically.

THE SIREN CALL

Perhaps more fascinating than the Appillionaires themselves is the mystery and allure surrounding the app business. It's become a siren call for thousands and thousands of amateur programmers and designers intent on living the App Store dream and becoming an overnight millionaire. One thing that stood out as I interviewed the app makers in this book: Often they discovered that complete strangers would stop and pitch them app ideas. Just as doctors find people asking them for medical diagnosis at a party, the app makers often find themselves in the middle of impromptu pitching sessions.

"I get pitched app ideas all the time. I got a phone call from a friend yesterday," explains Mills. "He said to me: 'You're an app man, I've got an idea for an app. I just don't know what to do. Should I patent it?,'" Mills sighs. "I said, 'What idea have you got?' Then he told me he wanted to go half-and-half. So, I would make the app based on his idea and he'd make half the money." Mills slams the table with his fist in anger. "I couldn't even answer him. What's the point?" Mills is clearly a man who has been pitched apps way beyond his tolerance point.

It seems that no sooner does a developer mention that he or she is in the app business than a crowd gathers and starts pitching app ideas, or asking how much he or she has made on the store. In this sense, the App Store increasingly does resemble a gold rush. It might be this overwhelming popular ambition to create apps that has caused a cynicism to take root. Tristan Celder, whose company, Zolmo, created the phenomenally successful *Jamie Oliver 20 Minute Meals* app, represents a growing number of developers who think that the gold rush is now largely a myth — perpetuated by the very developers who appear to be the richest.

"There's a lot of hype surrounding apps that Google and Apple are very good at manufacturing," explains Celder. "To be Apple's App of the Week looks like a stream of gold, but doesn't always come to fruition. There's a lot of young companies — start-ups — that are trying to inflate their own value to get investors, so they're happy for that hype to be there. But whenever someone isn't releasing download numbers, you have to wonder what's really going on."

WHY I WROTE *APPILLIONAIRES*

As you prod deeper into the world of the Appillionaires, the water gets increasingly murky, and that's precisely the reason I set out to write this book. Many of the people I've interviewed for Appillionaires have expressed confusion about the reality of the App Store, despite their massive successes. First, this book sets out to answer the biggest question on the technology scene today — What does it take to make a million dollars on the App Store? However, I also wanted to discover more about the other side of the App Store: Those who have struggled to find success.

It's this other side to the Appillionaire story that is almost more intriguing: The strange disparity between the amount of money actually made on the App Store and the public perception of the App Store as a goldmine. I wanted to discover, first-hand, if the Appillionaire dream was as widely realized as it appears to be. And, if it is indeed a rarity, how has the illusion of probable success been so widely and effectively spread by the mainstream media?

This impression of easy riches has been bolstered by newspapers and magazines, which seem to lap up every minor App Store success story with a mesmerizing eagerness. Apps have gone mainstream, pop-culture even: The masses have heard the apocryphal tales, the rags-to-riches stories, and they want to live the dream too. They wear *Angry Bird* T-shirts, and they tell each other increasingly ridiculous stories about the lavish houses of the programmer who built the wildly successful iShoot app. They draw game plans for world domination using *Sketchbook* on their iPads. But what is often forgotten, in the telling of these capitalist parables, is that few Appillionaires were true overnight successes.

> As Mills tells me of Angry Birds, "People say it was an overnight success. Well, yes, it was an overnight success after 52 other failed attempts."

WHERE WILL THE MARKET TAKE US?

Then there is the new wave of app makers. They're thinking bigger and they're better financed — some might say ridiculously financed. Apps like *Color,* which cost $41 million to launch, shocked the industry by demonstrating just how much raw cash investors were willing to throw at the mirage, but it was just the beginning. By April, the creators of an iPad app called *Flipboard*, a "social magazine," had managed to raise an investment of $50 million — valuing the company at $200 million. It's a staggering amount. *Flipboard* is a free app and though it dances around the very top of the iPad chart, at the time of writing it provides no tangible income for the company that built it. More worriesome still (for those that fear an app bubble is growing) is the justification for this enormous sum. *Flipboard's* CEO, Mike McCue, appeared to be channeling the venture capitalists who backed him when a journalist asked how the company could possibly need or want that much money.

Color, the most costly iPhone app built so far. It took a $41 million investment to launch the software. At the time of writing it has sunk down though the charts and user reviews of the app average two stars out of a possible five.

SOURCE: Copyright Color Inc.

"We decided the only way you could get to a multi-billion dollar business is through advertising. So given that, to build an advertising business, you've got to have a lot of scale. You've got to build a consumer brand, acquire tens of millions of users," McCue told TechCrunch in spring 2011.

This is the kind of language the app industry is beginning to use more and more often. The CEOs themselves have begun to echo the standard VC (venture capitalist) mantra to build it bigger and bigger, faster and faster. The VCs favorite word is scale, and although the tech industry has always attracted a legion of the wealthy and bewildered, the App Store has drummed up a mass of investment unseen since the dotcom boom. The Appillionaires have, through their success, spawned a climate where VCs circle greedily. In meetings with them, you can almost see the dollar signs spinning in their eyes. Armed with hedge-fund capital, and fresh from their MBA, they are the pinstriped wildebeest hunting for The Next Big Thing.

Max Slade from Johnny Two Shoes remembers the initial attack from VCs well. After the success of *Plunderland,* he had to take urgent action to fend them off.

"We actually unplugged our phone because we were getting so many calls from VCs saying, "We want to give you some money; let's give you some money. Here, have some money. Money. Money!" Slade tells me. He then mimes a grinning lunatic throwing out bundles of cash. Oddly, this is possibly the most accurate depiction I've witnessed of how investors react to an App Store success story. In the end, Slade declined to accept any VC cash.

This book also serves as an exposé of the app VCs and the people they hunt, desperate to invest their cash in the early stages of a your dream. They're eager to talk to young hopefuls like Andrew Lim who is, like me, a former journalist turned app developer.

Lim is trying to get venture capitalists interested in his new app idea. When I first asked him what his idea was he told me, "I'm making the next Face-book. Facebook Two, basically." He then burst into laughter. I told Lim it was possibly the least-convincing pitch I've ever heard.

"I've been talking to investors and I haven't been to a single pitch where I haven't burst out laughing or they haven't burst out laughing," Lim explained. "It is madness, but there's a small window of opportunity to make an impact. You've got crazy people coming into the app scene, there's ridiculous money out there and there'll be a crash. But there will also be a second spike, where it's all more refined."

THE BAND OF DREAMERS

In this book, you'll going to meet the rich, famous, and eccentric of the app development world. This unlikely band of dreamers includes the two brothers from Croatia who have sold over 10 million copies of *Doodle Jump*. The husband and wife team from Washington DC who made a fortune with their $1.99 app, *Harbor Master*. The studio behind *Angry Birds,* whose blockbuster app now looks likely to become a Hollywood feature film. And the makers of *Pocket God* and other smash-hit apps. You'll hear directly from these visionaries and learn their secrets first-hand. It's a weird and wonderful land where bedroom coders turn into millionaires overnight. Where teenaged code-monkeys flirt with venture capital and the good die young, iPhones in hand.

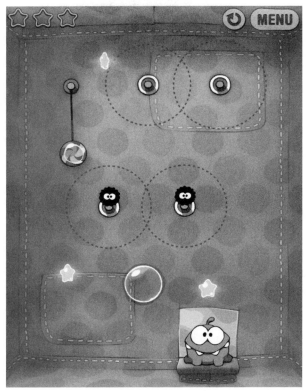

Cut the Rope is just one of many iOS success stories. It sold over one million copies just nine days into its release.

SOURCE: Copyright Chillingo Ltd.

In this book you're also going to meet the underdogs. The broken-hearted, the failures, and the disasters.

The rise of the app has massively altered the public perception of what a software programmer is. It's turned a generation of geeks from social misfits into superheroes. Mention to someone that you make iPhone apps and their interest will pick up instantly. They may even ask if you're a millionaire. This is an astonishing change from what a programmer in the 80s could have expected in reaction to their job description. We now live in an age where companies like Tapulous can, apparently without irony, run a job ad that reads, "We are hiring rock-star developers." Amazingly, if you visit a modern development studio, you may find that the workers are treated a bit like rock stars. The demand for good programmers has never been greater and this is reflected in the perks being offered to entice them to new start-ups.

SUMMARY

A good iPhone programmer is rare and much in demand. The geek-kings you'll learn about in this book have become increasingly aware of their value. The Appillionaires have encouraged a new breed of programmers, born in their image, who are edging toward the golden days of the dotcom bubble — a time when technology geniuses could entrance docile investors with promises of glory. Riding around your Soho loft on a kid's plastic tricycle while the head of marketing squirts you with a water pistol has become socially acceptable again. We live in crazy times.

Here's a roundup of the important points covered in this chapter:

- The cost of playing the Appillionaire game is theoretically low. It's just $99 to join up as an Apple developer. The real expense is the investment of your time, or paying people's salaries.

- Over $250 million is spent at the Apple App Store every month. And it's just the start. The mobile software industry is witnessing explosive growth.

- Even successful developers recognize an element of luck is involved in building a hit app. There are few guarantees.

- Apple has complete editorial control over what goes on the App Store. The Appillionaires have to work within the bounds of what Apple considers acceptable material for sale, both technically and morally.

■ Hysterical venture capitalists are investing huge amounts of money into the app scene right now. There couldn't be a better time to seek investment for your grand scheme. Just make sure you have a back-up plan in case things turn apocalyptic — they probably will.

Now you know the basic geography of the Appillionaire's universe, let's take a trip through the door of the world's most mysterious, alluring, and nonsensical shop: The Apple App Store.

2

THE RISE OF THE APP

"TURN ON THE iPhone and the first, and only, thing you see is apps. When the iPhone came out it was striking that everything, everything, was an app. Even the voice call functionality was encapsulated in an app. This was a massive departure from phones at the time, which all had Send and End buttons. The mobile phone had been a physical thing and the iPhone made it a software app." — John Gruber, Daring Fireball.

It's September 7, 2005, and Steve Jobs is standing on stage at San Francisco's Moscone Center to unveil a phone. It is the same stage he'll take to in 2007 to launch the iPhone, but Jobs is here today to launch a very different product — a product that will bear very little relation to the iPhone. It is a new cell phone, built by Apple in collaboration with Motorola. The new phone is called the Motorola Rokr, and it includes an iTunes music player. But the device is remarkably un-Apple like; it looks clumsy and complex. When Jobs attempts to take a call on the phone, it doesn't work properly, failing to continue playing music when the call is ended.

"Well," Jobs says, staring in confusion at the phone, "I'm supposed to be able to resume the music right back to where it was." The audience is silent. "Oops! I hit the wrong button."

APPLE'S FALSE START

Apple's first, desperately flawed attempt at building a phone has faded into history, but the company's experience with Motorola was crucial in bringing about the iPhone and provoking the global rise of the app. Apple's failed collaboration with Motorola gave Jobs a chance to peek behind the curtain at the inner workings of the cell phone industry and, most importantly, it confirmed Apple's deepest suspicion: The cell phone carriers didn't have a clue. The industry was wrecking cell phones through a lethal combination of greed and laziness. The traditional cell phone companies were not interested in providing an enjoyable user experience because they profited so much from customers locked in to contracts and paying tolls for every additional service.

The Motorola Rokr

SOURCE: Reproduced with
permission of Motorola Inc.
© 2011 Motorola Inc.

The Motorola Razr

SOURCE: Reproduced with permission
of Motorola Inc. © 2011 Motorola Inc.

Back in 2005, the cell phone industry was cut throat. Rumors abounded that cell phone carriers had threatened Motorola, telling the company that if it sold the Rokr, they would cease stocking Motorola phones in their stores. Even in the horribly crippled state iTunes existed in on the Rokr, it was seen as a threat to the carriers. The kings and crooks of a U.S. industry that raked in over $11 billion a year would not stand for it. The giant cell phone networks resented the idea that customers might buy music through iTunes, paying Apple without paying anything to the carrier. In this atmosphere, there was simply no motivation for most manufacturers to improve phone hardware and software because the carriers would throttle them at every twist and turn. Even Apple, fresh from the success of the iMac and iPod, could not create something great among such hostility and entrenched players. The Rokr was a dud.

THE MYSTERY OF THE MOTOROLA FIASCO

Although it's tempting to recast Apple's relationship with Motorola as an information-gathering exercise for Apple before the company attempted its own phone, the likelihood is that Apple genuinely had high expectations for its collaboration with Motorola. Back in 2005, Motorola was riding high on the success of the Razr, a beautifully designed and fiercely popular phone that sold over 110 million handsets. The Razr looked every bit an Apple product and, to Apple's design team in Cupertino, Motorola must have seemed an extremely attractive partner.

The eventual reality of this collaboration was tragically different: Although the Razr was a visionary design that stuck to a simple purpose and did it well, the Rokr was an embarrassing mess. As an iPod-cellphone hybrid it offered the worst of both worlds: It was capable of storing only 100 songs and couldn't even download music directly from the Internet. It also lacked the most popular feature of Apple's successful iPod: the click wheel. The Rokr had no way to scroll quickly through songs — although given that it could only store 100 of them, there was hardly any point anyway. If two manufacturers had set out to produce a phone that exemplified the failures of the industry, they could hardly have produced something more ugly and incapable than the Rokr. The reviewers at CNET called it "a dull design" and described the interface as "sluggish," while PC Magazine proclaimed it "clumsy."

The sad fact was that even when the world's most innovative computer manufacturer and one of the world's leading phone companies attempted to collaborate, they still got it wrong. The conflict between hardware manufacturers and the carriers whose networks they were granted permission to use was too great. It almost seemed as if Motorola's engineers were actively censoring their own innovation to avoid angering these hugely powerful cartels of the airwaves. It also appeared that the earlier success of the Razr was a fluke, and no indication of Motorola's ongoing commitment to great design.

Apple quickly distanced themselves from the project. Jon Rubinstein, senior vice president at iPod Division, would come to dismiss the Rokr as simply "an experiment."

Motorola were not so gracious in defeat. CEO Ed Zander fell into a fury. Just three weeks after the launch of the Rokr, he raged against the popularity of the iPod Nano, telling MacWorld, "Screw the Nano. What the hell does the Nano do? Who listens to 1,000 songs? People are going to want devices that do more than just play music, something that can be seen in many other countries with more advanced mobile phone networks and savvy users."

Zander was right, but Motorola wasn't going to be anywhere in sight when this revolution began.

IF AT FIRST YOU DON'T SUCCEED…

The failure of the Motorola Rokr collaboration taught Steve Jobs an important lesson, a lesson that would lead directly to the invention of the most profitable phone in history: If Apple were going to make a phone, they would have to do it alone. They would have to do it largely without the permission of the carriers, and without the help of any phone manufacturer. Even if it meant a radical step as like setting themselves up as a carrier, Apple was determined to break through.

After the Motorola fiasco, Jobs began to publically express his resentment of the U.S. cell phone market. He was so outspoken in his hostility towards the idea of making another phone that few would have guessed what Apple were cooking up in their Cupertino labs at the time. Jobs repeatedly denied that Apple was working on a phone, yet while he poured scorn on the state of the cell phone industry, Apple engineers were quietly working on a top-secret project to build a new breed of cell phone without the endorsement of the carriers.

"We're not very good going through orifices to get to the end users; we've never been real good at that," explained Jobs at the All Things Digital conference in 2005.

> *"The carriers now have gained the upper hand in terms of the power of the relationship with the handset manufacturer, and they're telling the handset manufacturer what to build. The handset manufactures are getting these big thick books saying what you're phone is going to be."*

Jobs talked orifices on one hand while, on the other, Cupertino quietly learned everything it could about building phones. Apple's campus became a hive of activity, but as with Wonka's Chocolate Factory, the gates remained shut and it was almost as if nobody ever went in and nobody ever came out. Unknown to the rest of Silicon Valley, around 200 Apple employees were set to work on a new phone, a phone that would be designed and built in secret, far away from the cartels of the cell phone industry. But the phone design was so secret that many of Apple's own engineers did not know exactly what it was they were working on. The iPhone project was carefully compartmentalized so that the designers who worked on the iPhone software could not physically see the hardware they were programming for. While, in other rooms on the Apple campus, many hardware designers worked on circuits that were running dummy software that did not resemble the finished product.

In Apple's opinion, the industry couldn't be trusted to build a decent phone, so Apple was going to show them how it was done. It was risky — perhaps pure lunacy given the stranglehold of the carriers — but Apple had never shied from impossible tasks before. Decades of war with Microsoft had hardened the company to taking on giants.

TAKING A JOURNEY BACK IN TIME

It's interesting to revisit, from a software-design perspective, what the cell phone industry was like back in 2005. Although the touchscreen is incredibly popular today, there were no touchscreen-only phones in 2005. Mobile phone interfaces were almost universally reviled by consumers who found the simplest operations would mean tapping buttons in odd combinations and scrolling through many layers of menus.

A typical mobile phone menu
system in 2005

SOURCE: Reproduced with
permission of Nokia © 2011 Nokia.

The major cell phone engineers, disillusioned by the carriers, had fallen into a rut. A kind of unspoken agreement seemed to exist between the leading manufacturers: Why bother to make any phone better than any other when it was ultimately the giant carriers who would dictate what phone people upgraded to? The industry was trapped in a stand-off: Because handsets were subsidized, phone manufacturers were effectively selling their products to the carriers, not to the end consumer. The result was that phones were sold on the basis of boardroom deals, not consumer preferences. From the perspective of these huge businesses, the situation was ideal. There was no risk if a cell phone company failed to innovate, because the consumer had no choice but to accept one of the phone handsets the carrier pushed in front of them every six months.

FINDING A CARRIER WAS THE THING

Apple saw a way to break this cycle; what it desperately needed was a way into the carrier's club. Building an iPhone was one thing, but whose network would they use? What carrier in their right mind would let a brand-new cell phone manufacturer upset its entire industry? Who would allow an upstart like Apple to dictate terms?

Engineering the iPhone hardware was difficult enough, but convincing a carrier to give Apple the control it needed over the design of the iPhone would be even harder. After months of secret meetings with AT&T executives, Jobs somehow managed to achieve the unthinkable: Apple would have total control over the hardware and software design of the iPhone, in exchange for five years of exclusive iPhone sales for AT&T.

Looking back today, given the success of the iPhone, this might appear like a spectacular deal for AT&T, but in 2007 it was unheard of for a carrier to cede control of a phone and its software. The entire industry operated on the basis that cell phones were heavily subsidized — leased at a loss to customers — and then profits were made by tying customers into proprietary services: call charges, Internet access, ringtones, and the like. Apple convinced AT&T that these services should be bundled with the contract and the phone hardware paid for at its true cost.

Apple's initial motivation may have been to create a well-designed phone, free of the tasteless intervention of the carriers. But the company's unprecedented deal with AT&T had an unexpected repercussion — two years later it would lead directly to the birth of the App Store. The unbundling of the iPhone's hardware from the carriers' control meant that Apple would soon be allowed to try its hand at selling software to cell phone users directly.

The app revolution had begun.

SUMMARY

Here's a roundup of the important points covered in this chapter:

- Apple's first attempt to build a phone, the Motorola Rokr, was a complete failure. But the company learned an important lesson: they would have to work *alone*.
- The iPhone was designed in response to the carrier-focused model of cell phone sales. Apple decided to ignore the restrictions of the carriers and attempt to sell a phone that appealed exclusively to the consumer.

- The iPhone was designed and built in complete secrecy. Only a few hundred trusted employees knew the project existed.
- Apple's unique deal with AT&T allowed Apple complete control over the software and features of the iPhone. This was the first time that a hardware manufacturer had dictated terms to a carrier. Usually the carrier would have forced subscribers to pay for many of the services Apple decided should be bundled by default.

3

A BEDROOM REVOLUTION

"STEVE JOBS TOLD *USA Today* that the Apple App Store will launch with "more than 500 apps"... Of these, 25 percent will be free and 90 percent (of those for sale) will cost $9.99 or less. "This is the biggest launch of my career," said Jobs. Analyst Tim Bajarin at Creative Strategies said, "When IBM introduced the PC, it was good, but it didn't take off until people started discovering the software." It's these apps then, he adds, that "dramatically differentiates the iPhone" from Treos and BlackBerrys. Indeed, while consumers are focused on the launch of the iPhone 3G device, it's the App Store which has analysts in such a tizzy." — Thomas Ricker — Engadget

BIRTH OF THE APP STORE

It's testament to the cleverness of any great idea that once it exists, you can hardly imagine things any other way. The App Store has become such an influential part of the mobile phone scene that it's difficult to imagine what things were like before the app explosion, or to rationalize the extremely short amount of time in which the app business has taken over the tech industry.

Amazingly, the first iPhone did not launch with an App Store. The App Store is a relatively recent invention, unleashed on July 11th, 2008, but in that time it has come to dominate both the mobile industry and popular culture itself. For a company that sells a tiny percentage of the mobile phones on the planet, Apple takes the majority share of the profits. So, not only does the App Store have influence beyond its users, but the devices through which apps are sold — the iPhone, iPod Touch, and the iPad — have defied what was thought to be a basic capitalist tenet: to make the most profit you must sell the most of a given product. Apple demonstrated, bizarrely, that you could make a hell of a lot more money by selling less.

Homebrew Apps Came First

Back in 2007, before the announcement of the official Apple App Store, demand for iPhone apps was so great that a "homebrew" community of hackers reverse engineered the iPhone software and created their own apps. These apps could be installed only if the users were prepared to "jail-break" their iPhones — download a piece of software that accessed the iPhone at a low level to permit third-party apps. The enthusiasm behind this movement was extraordinary, and all the more impressive an accomplishment given that these homebrew hackers did not have access to documentation, or to the iPhone SDK (Software Development Kit) — this is the software that lets programmers design apps for Apple devices. These early pioneers of the app created some very polished games and utilities that look similar to what is available on the official App Store today. That they managed this without any help from Apple was an early indication of just how desperate users were to get their hands on apps, and how keen programmers were to create them. By October 2007, the homebrew app store, called Cydia, had grown so popular that Steve Jobs took the unusual step of pre-announcing an Apple product: The official Apple App Store was on its way.

"Let me just say it: We want native third-party applications on the iPhone, and we plan to have an SDK in developers' hands in February. We are excited about creating a vibrant third-party developer community around the iPhone and enabling hundreds of new applications for our users. It will take until February to release an SDK because we're trying to do two diametrically opposed things at once — provide an advanced and open platform to developers while at the same time protect iPhone users from viruses, malware, privacy attacks, etc. As our phones become more powerful, these malicious programs will become more dangerous, and since the iPhone is the most advanced phone ever, it will be a highly visible target. We think a few months of patience now will be rewarded by many years of great third-party applications running on safe and reliable iPhones," wrote Jobs.

Stranger still is the story of how the App Store came to be. As with many stories involving Apple, the definitive truth is difficult to uncover. The company thrives on a culture of secrecy that has worked extremely well for it in keeping a step ahead of their competition and in building anticipation for future products. We can be reasonably sure, however, that the success of the App Store took Apple by surprise — 100 million app downloads were achieved in the first three months and then double that just one month later. As Steve Jobs explained at a 2008 Apple earnings call, "We've never seen anything like this in our careers."

Initially the App Store contained a meager 550 apps, one third of them games (some things never change), but the store had increased its stock to over 800 apps by the end of launch week. This was the tiniest hint of things to come: In the months to follow there would be a supernatural fervor from app developers; an explosion of interest in mobile phone software and the rebirth of the bedroom programmer. Finally, with the iPhone, there was a mass-market software platform and a low bar to entry for creatives — $99 to sign up as an iPhone developer — and there were also millions of potential customers who had already supplied Apple with their credit card information through iTunes.

It's no exaggeration to state that for the first time in history, thousands of garage programmers and designers were suddenly given direct access to the mass market — an App Store purchase was one finger-tap away from millions of consumers. For a brief moment, it no longer mattered if you were as big as Disney, or simply one human, alone in the light of your computer screen, everyone was on equal footing. There was still a gatekeeper, and an unpredictable one at that — Apple — but for all its demands, the company would operate a much more egalitarian system than what went before. It was no longer the suits at Warner Bros or Random House who decided whether your music or writing was worthy of global distribution.

A RETAIL MAGIC TRICK

Many of the barriers that had made the Internet a haphazard nightmare for small-publishers evaporated. Because Apple already held the credit card details of millions of iTunes users, and these users already trusted Apple, it was possible for one app to make a fortune from thousands of very small transactions. This was the micro-payment dream repeatedly promised in the Internet age, and finally it had arrived: except it wasn't happening on the

Internet per-se, it was happening in the App Store. It seemed that people were willing to pay small one-off sums for low-cost, single-purpose applications as long as it was to Apple, a company they trusted, through iTunes. It's easy to under-estimate the retail magic-trick Apple pulled off with the App Store: They effectively used the same payment system that millions were using to buy music, and applied it to software. What seems blindingly obvious now was once a completely alien concept.

WHAT APPLE LEARNED FROM THE FIRST SUCCESSFUL APPS

By the end of 2008, over 300 million apps had been downloaded by iPhone owners and the App Store was brimming with more than 10,000 apps — so many that Apple struggled to keep up with the backlog of submissions waiting to be vetted before they were allowed into the store, a problem that would continue to plague the company for many years. Although some of the top-sellers were familiar brands like *Super Monkey Ball* (Sega) and Crash *Bandicoot Nitro Kart 3D* (Vivendi Games Mobile), many others were true indie success stories. There was *Koi Pond* (Shinya Kasatani), borne of a relatively simple idea: to create a simulation of a Japanese water feature. Users could tap their fingers on the iPhone screen to make the pond ripple and briefly scare the Koi fish away. The result was hypnotic and oddly addictive.

Then there were apps that have now attained a legendary status, apps like *iBeer* (Hottrix), which creates the illusion that the iPhone is a small glass of beer which, when tilted towards the user's open mouth, appears to be swallowed down.

iBeer was a runaway success and is likely responsible for selling more iPhones than any other app to date. It took a simple, human concept — drinking beer — and married it to one of the iPhone's most obviously unique features: the accelerometer (a circuit inside the phone that allows the device to detect the angle at which it is being held). This accelerometer feature was fairly complex to visualize based purely on a spec sheet, then one day it was suddenly glaringly obvious to the masses what the accelerometer was for: It was for fun. You could pull your phone out in a bar and pretend to your friends that you were drinking a beer. Steve Jobs surely shuddered at the crassness of it all, but what better advertisement for the company's new phone than to have Apple's customers showing the device off at every opportunity.

Koi Pond simulated rare tropical fish. The app was an early success on the App Store.

SOURCE: Reproduced with permission of Brandon Bogle © 2011 The Blimp Pilots.

With the success of *iBeer* came two interesting discoveries. One: That a very simple and inexpensive app could make an Appillionaire of its creator. Two: That apps could sell iPhones. Lots of iPhones. Popular apps encouraged users to share the experiences they had with the iPhone hardware. They would show off *iBeer,* and other apps, to non-Apple-users, who might then go on to buy an iPhone.

iBeer let iPhone users create the illusion that they were drinking a glass of beer.

SOURCE: Reproduced with permission of Hottrix © 2011 Hottrix.

THE DEVELOPER COMMUNITY GROWS

Apple's realization that popular apps could sell more iPhone hardware led to the company's increased investment in the developer community. By 2009, Apple was approving 95 percent of app submissions in under 14 days, no mean feat given the volume of apps being created. Anyone who believes that Apple's relationship with developers is restricted to rejecting apps has been misled by the press coverage given to these events — in fact, a very small percentage of apps are rejected for objectionable content — around 10 percent.

"We review the applications to make sure they work as the customers expect them to work when they download them. We've built a store for the most part that people can trust," Apple senior vice president for worldwide product marketing, Phil Schiller explained to *Businessweek* in 2009. "You and your family and friends can download applications from the store, and for the most part they do what you'd expect, and they get onto your phone, and you get billed appropriately, and it all just works."

Nobody talks very much about the good Apple does for developers, and to an extent Apple likes it that way, preferring to operate in secrecy. Many developers are reluctant to discuss the ways in which Apple helps them to achieve success in the App Store — the Appillionaires rely on Apple for their livelihood and would rather not risk angering the world's most notoriously private corporation by revealing too much. I'll return to this topic later.

PROFITS AND DOWNLOADS GROW

"Thanks a billion. Over one billion downloads in just nine months," Apple announced in April 2009. The App Store had reached a giant milestone, with users collectively downloading approximately 5.1 million apps every day. An astonishing 97 percent of iPhone owners had downloaded at least one app, more than 43 percent had downloaded more than 10 apps and 17 percent had downloaded 31 or more apps. If there was ever any doubt that Apple had begun a revolution in computer software, that doubt had now evaporated. By the middle of that same year, 1.5 billion apps had been downloaded by Apple users and the App Store was now home to over 65,000 apps created by some of the 100,000 programmers now signed up to the iPhone Developer Program. Two months later, Apple had shifted another 500,000 downloads and an average of 65 apps had been downloaded for every iPhone and iPod Touch sold so far. Apple had now reached a total of 85,000 apps in the store.

Free apps accounted for 65-70 percent of the software installed on iPhones in 2009, which meant that an impressive proportion were paid apps, with 99¢ already established as the most popular price. By the end of 2009, Apple had supplied over 2 billion apps to iPhone and iPod Touch users in 77 different countries, netting developers over $900 million. Customers were downloading an average of 11 apps each per month and a mind-boggling 8,500 new apps were being submitted to Apple by programmers every week.

GROWING PAINS

The popularity of the App Store was now at risk of spoiling Apple's carefully self-managed image as a poster child of liberal thinking. The company's role as gatekeeper was a significant reason for the success of the App Store — Google would quickly discover the mess that resulted from a store that was not curated. But Apple put itself in a tricky position as moral arbiter. It has confronted everyone from outright criminals and pornographers, through to political cartoonists, rivals, and people who they just didn't like much, to prevent them from selling apps on the store.

The danger of taking up the role of curating the App Store has often put Apple in conflict with its own ideals. Jobs himself places Apple at the "intersection of technology and liberal arts." But there are many unsettling examples of the company's conflicted motivations. The controversy over Pulitzer Prize-winning cartoonist Mark Fiore's app *NewsToons* is just one example of the difficult responsibility Apple faces as a curator.

NewsToons was initially rejected from the App Store in 2010, for "obscene, pornographic, offensive, or defamatory content." In reality it contained nothing more than political satire. The resulting outcry in the press convinced Apple to reconsider the app and eventually approve it. On the face of things, it might seem that the App Store approval system, although clumsy, ultimately works. But, as The Register editorialized at the time, "To gain admission into the iTunes App Store, a political commentator shouldn't have to win a Pulitzer Prize."

> *By the middle of 2010, just over 80 percent of apps downloaded were free, and yet developers had earned more than $1 billion from selling paid apps.*

The analysts at Munster estimated that Apple's profit from the App Store, after credit card processing fees, was $189 million — the company takes a 30 percent share of every app sold. Compare this to Apple's $33.7 billion profit from its entire business during the lifetime of the App Store up to this point in 2010 and a curious picture develops: The App Store accounts for barely 1 percent of Apple's profits. Yet it is a focal point for the media, and has by virtue of its success, provoked the purchase of thousands of iPhones. By the end of 2010, Apple had announced the sale of over 120 million iPhones, iPods, and iPad devices and also revealed that the company activated over 230,000 new devices every day. To deal with the extraordinary influx of new app submissions, Apple published the App Store Review Guidelines.

ENTER THE APP STORE REVIEW GUIDELINES

"We have over 250,000 apps in the App Store. We don't need any more Fart apps… If your app doesn't do something useful or provide some form of lasting entertainment, it may not be accepted… If your App looks like it was cobbled together in a few days, or you're trying to get your first practice app into the store to impress your friends, please brace yourself for rejection. We have lots of serious developers who don't want their quality apps to be surrounded by amateur hour… We will reject apps for any content or behavior that we believe is over the line… What line, you ask? Well, as a Supreme Court Justice once said, 'I'll know it when I see it.' And we think that you will also know it when you cross it," the document says.

A RENAISSANCE IN GAMING

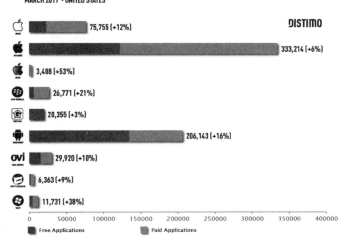

NUMBER OF AVAILABLE APPLICATIONS
MARCH 2011 - UNITED STATES

DISTIMO

75,755 (+12%)

333,214 (+6%)

3,408 (+53%)

26,771 (+21%)

20,355 (+3%)

206,143 (+16%)

29,920 (+10%)

6,363 (+9%)

11,731 (+38%)

| 0 | 50000 | 100000 | 150000 | 200000 | 250000 | 300000 | 350000 | 400000 |

■ Free Applications   ■ Paid Applications

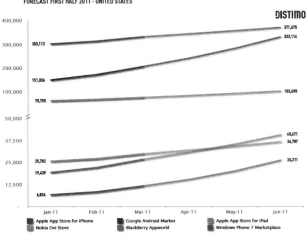

FUTURE DEVELOPMENTS IN THE APP STORE ECOSYSTEM
FORECAST FIRST HALF 2011 - UNITED STATES

DISTIMO

■ Apple App Store for iPhone   ■ Google Android Market   ■ Apple App Store for iPad
■ Nokia Ovi Store   ■ BlackBerry Appworld   ■ Windows Phone 7 Marketplace

Graph showing the rapid explosion in iPhone app sales.

Today, users have downloaded well over 10 billion apps from the store and the developer community surrounding the iPhone is the biggest in the world. Despite the store's massive success, the cost to play the development game remains at $99. Every day more and more wild-eyed dreamers sign up to try their hand at the App Store dream: to build a hit app, usually a game. The iPhone's relative simplicity, and the way it has historically rewarded very basic, casual game formats, makes it an extremely attractive proposition to anyone with a biro and a napkin handy.

Just five years ago videogame and application design seemed so profoundly inaccessible to the layman that it was idiocy to attempt to build a software company around an idea like *Angry Birds, Tiny Wings,* or *Cut the Rope.* But the reality of micropayment transactions through iTunes, combined with a pocket-sized device with enough power to run basic apps — the iPhone — has completely changed the landscape of software engineering. Game design made a transition away from expensive, complex, 3D titles (as is still required for platforms like the PlayStation and Xbox) and towards cheap, simple 2D gaming.

As the iPhone encouraged an aesthetic shift back towards the 2D, it brought with it a renaissance of mechanic-driven gameplay familiar to Commodore 64 or Atari owners: a simpler, arguably more enjoyable game experience that did not require hours of learning and immersion to reward the players. The mainstream gaming companies like Sony and Microsoft had spent a fortune building the videogames industry into a replica of the film business, but Apple would undo it all in a matter of months.

Prior to the iPhone, the industry was almost exclusively fixated on massive titles that they worked on for years, with budgets stretching into the millions. It was the most effective way to make money — or so they thought. But the iPhone demonstrated that the mainstream console manufacturers had abandoned casual gamers. The masses wanted cheap, straightforward games they could dip in and out of during a bored moment on the train. They didn't necessarily want a virtual film experience with layered plots and an advanced control system; they just wanted the next *Tetris*. Although the videogames giants initially shrugged their shoulders at the iPhone and carried on, it eventually became hard to ignore the effect Apple's device was having on the public. By the spring of 2011, two of Nintendo's leading marketing executives had abandoned the gaming monolith and joined Apple. The heart of gaming had clearly made a shift into the pockets of millions of iPhone-toting youngsters.

App development that once cost millions could now be undertaken by a single dedicated individual working alone with enough spare cash to buy food for a month or two. The threat was enormous, and nobody saw it coming.

SUMMARY

Here's a roundup of the important points covered in this chapter:

- The scale of the App Store's success came as a surprise, even to Apple.
- Garage programmers were instantly drawn to the App Store. The $99 price of entry was low, and these developers were put on equal footing with large corporations. The App Store is as close to a meritocracy as the software world has seen yet.
- With the success of the App Store, Apple has taken on a difficult role as gatekeeper and moral arbiter for the content on the store. In exchange for a safe shopping environment, users can only purchase software that has passed Apple's rigorous and infamous reviews process. Every app on the store is vetted by Apple's own hand.
- The App Store has provoked a renaissance in gaming, especially games that prize fun and enjoyment over graphical complexity. The limitations of the iPhone hardware and the touch-input mechanism are restrictions that have inspired a new generation of programmers.

4 THE GOLD RUSH

"THE ANTICIPATION WAS almost too much to handle. We'd made £11,000 in a single day. We didn't know what to do. We got really confused and ended up losing the plot, with excitement and shock. We'd let this app out into the wild and watched it go. I sat in front of *Magic Rank,* watching the profits go up and up. We were buzzing off it. I remember not knowing what would happen next; when the end would be. Nothing made sense. We couldn't take it. We just shut down. I took a week off and did nothing, just stared at a wall. I had to stop looking at stats, completely. I couldn't sleep at all, just frazzled. You know how when you've had too much coffee and your brain goes mad? It was like that for a week and a half. Just so buzzed. It's that feeling of being successful. This directly affected our lives. Just two people did this." — Max Slade, one half of Johnny Two Shoes who, with his brother Josh, created the smash hit app *Plunderland.*

A TASTE OF SUCCESS

I know first-hand the extraordinary rush of creating a global hit on the App Store. I was one half of the two-person team that created *Alice* for the iPad. The book became so popular that it was a star guest on the Oprah Winfrey show in the week the iPad launched in the United States. Watching your app being shown off by Oprah is hard to do without screaming and clapping: the buzz was gut wrenching. It was a realization of the dream that every developer hopes for when they sign up to the App Store. Almost as soon as *Alice* hit the number one spot I was fielding calls from *The New York Times,* giving interviews to Japanese television stations, and advising major print publishers on how to make digital books. *Alice* was literally programmed in a bedroom — a phenomena that the App Store had made possible — and, for a brief moment I was the most famous Appillionaire on the planet.

What few people saw were the months of near insanity that led up to the success of *Alice.* The confusion and self-doubt as app after app that we attempted to sell on the App Store failed to turn a profit. Alice was the culmination of almost a year of repeated failures. We were so sure about our first app, *Twitch Origins* — a four-player game for the iPhone — that when it failed to sell more than a few dozen copies I was tempted to walk away from the App Store forever and live in a tent. At the time, I was working day shifts at a newspaper in London, so the only time I could spend designing apps was limited to nights. What made things even more difficult was that the programmer on *Alice* was based in Seattle, thousands of miles away and in a completely different time zone. Just before I went to sleep, I would check in and explain the designs I'd completed to the programmer, Ben Roberts, at which point he would then take over. No other business in the world would let you run a major programming project over Skype across time zones, but it worked out for us.

Just as Roberts was running out of money to pay his rent and I was about to surrender to the painful reality that the App Store had defeated us, *Alice* went supernova. Overnight we were a global sensation — newspapers and blogs all over the world were hailing us as the future of publishing. Watching the money roll in and the download statistics rise became a minor obsession. There's something wildly captivating about viewing your successes through the microscope of modern analytic software. Second by second, hour by hour. It provokes a kind of statistic fetishism where viewing download graphs by geographical region or time of day becomes an opportunity to self-indulgently wallow in your accomplishment. We've never lived in an age so supplicant to the human ego. Whether it's the number of friends you have on Facebook, your Twitter followers, or views of your videos on YouTube, there's an almost infinite flow of metrics by which to judge your worth as a human being.

The smash-hit *Alice for the iPad*. Versions of the book are installed on over 500,000 iPads.

SOURCE: Reproduced with permission of Atomic Antelope LTD © 2011 Atomic Antelope Ltd.

FEELING THE APPILLIONAIRE BUZZ

Around 3am the day after *Alice* made us a fortune I finally switched the computer off, stared at myself in the mirror, and wondered what the hell I had become. The App Store had established some kind of intravenous connection to my body and was pumping me full of Apple-branded heroin. More people than I could actually visualize — hundreds of thousands of people — were playing with a book we created and, what's more, they were paying for it. The thought sent me into the throes of a weird manic episode caused by people I didn't know tapping the Buy button next to *Alice* on their iPad screens. This was my first taste of the Appillionaire buzz, and it's a feeling that's since been described to me by many of the people I interviewed for this book. The Appillionaire buzz is more powerful than anything on the streets. It's a hugely enjoyable sense of excitement mixed with satisfaction, but it is a disgusting sight to behold: a man cradled in the arms of his own ego being rocked to sleep.

It's this sensation, or the aspiration to feel this sensation and the financial rewards that come with it, that drives many people to create apps for Apple devices. However, I'm not cynical enough to believe that it's the only reason. There is pleasure to be had from the simple act of creating a product and selling it. However, an increasing number of entrepreneurs have begun looking to the App Store purely to cash in on the amazing popularity of mobile applications.

THE FALLACY OF EASY MONEY

Although the term "gold rush" was initially used by the press as a simple label for the sheer volume of developers flocking to the iPhone platform, it has recently become an oddly prescient historical reference point for the way the app scene is developing. The store has become a magnet for the overly optimistic with money to spend on getting their app built. I've sat in meeting after meeting with recent university graduates who have scraped together thousands of pounds from friends and family with the intention of making a fortune on the App Store. Almost without fail their ideas have been vague, or based on gut instinct, rather than the commercial realities of the world's most competitive software market. The illusion persists that there's gold in the hills but, for the majority, there is nothing but dust. It's a reality that seasoned developers are only too familiar with.

> *"Lots of people are starting out on their own and seeing if they can make it on the App Store, which is great," says Tristan Celder. "But it's an emerging industry and [big companies] will begin to look at the science of making money on the App Store to a point where they figure out the formulas and begin pushing out [the hobbyists]. They will consolidate and the bedroom programmers may have to join bigger companies if they want to make money."*

What then has caused this huge chasm between the average programmers experience on the App Store and the public's opinion that apps are easy money? Most likely it is the gap between the cost of building an app and the potential reward. Just like a casino, app developers are aware that the majority of apps fail, but there remains a glimmer of hope that they could be the one; that this time the winning hand will be theirs. It's a sense of hope compounded by the media's love affair with Apple's products.

The Love Affair with Apple

In fairness, Apple has earned the respect of the press. Every Apple launch is closely followed not just because of the excitement surrounding the newest technology, but because Apple tends to dictate the direction of the whole industry: to watch where Apple is heading now is to know where Microsoft, HP, or Sony is heading tomorrow. It's hard for journalists to keep their eyes off the company. Articles, books, and shows about successful people are much more popular than stories about losers, and so the press loves to write about Apple. The popular narrative of the App Store often continues unabated — you can make a million dollars!

In the next chapter I'm going to take a look at the brutal realities of the App Store, but also the spectacular successes. You'll learn the cold fiscal truth of what many developers invest, and lose, on the App Store. But, like me, you're probably a sucker for the big dream and are likely to ignore the failures and concentrate on the successes — there's plenty of those too.

The eternal conundrum of whether to get off the sofa and accomplish something lingers: Try and you will likely fail; do nothing and you'll definitely fail. The App Store is a creative litmus test for the idea you've always wanted to act on. Now, let's play the game.

SUMMARY

Here's a roundup of the important points covered in this chapter:

- Achieving a top-selling app on the store is an overwhelming buzz. It combines the thrill of accomplishment with the raw financial reward. You might just lose your mind for a while in the process.

- A few very public successes have created the impression that the App Store is an easy competitive landscape. In reality, it's a very tough market. Nevertheless a "gold rush" has occurred and creatives across the world are keen to get involved in the scene.

- The media is enamored with Apple as a company — and for good reason — but it's often difficult to get a fair and realistic picture of what life is like for the majority of developers on the store. Many low-profile developers are doing very well with moderate, steady incomes. Many more barely cover their costs. A lucky few are Appillionaires.

5

THE FIRST MILLION

IN THE SUMMER of 2007, the future Appillionaires were faced with a big problem: The iPhone didn't do apps.

At launch, the iPhone did not have the ability to install any new software at all — users were stuck with a single screen of simple utilities that Apple bundled with the phone. There was Mail, Calculator, Safari, and others, but it was impossible to add new icons to the iPhone, or remove the existing ones — in fact the very idea of "apps" for the iPhone was entirely hypothetical. The App Store didn't exist and, as far as the user could tell, the original iPhone was as immutable as a DVD player or television. You tapped a button and the iPhone switched mode, becoming a calculator, a telephone, or a calendar, but the iPhone's capabilities were limited only to what Apple had prescribed and nothing more. There were, however, hints that something more exciting lurked under the hood.

A BOX OF DELIGHTS

It was already well known that the iPhone was running some variant of Apple's OSX (the software used on Apple desktop computers) and this suggested that it could be possible to run extremely advanced software on the device. But back in the summer of 2007, exactly what was going on under the hood of the iPhone was a complete mystery to anyone outside the Cupertino campus. Steve Jobs had always said that software was the key ingredient of any great hardware design, but as yet there was no way for users to install new software on the iPhone, or for programmers outside of Apple to create it.

It was also clear to many developers that the iPhone was the most advanced pocket-sized computer ever produced — and certainly the first mass-market touchscreen device with a UNIX operating system (a favorite of the hacker community). With the iPhone, Apple had inadvertently created super-powerful hacker bait. Coders all over the world could not wait to get inside and figure out what made the device tick. Within days of its launch, the race was on to crack the iPhone.

Hackers all over the world decided they would attempt to provide iPhone owners with a set of tools to allow them to unlock their iPhones and install third-party software. This jail-break community operated in a grey area outside Apple's control.

Their success in opening up the iPhone to indie programmers would ultimately shape the future of the App Store.

Several of today's hit iPhone games began life as unsanctioned apps — games like *Tap Tap Revenge* — and the Appillionaires owe much of their success to this pioneering few who dared tinker with their expensive new iPhones to install software. At the time, the work of these hackers seemed little more than a curiosity, but it would ultimately change everything, giving developers an early taste of programming for what would later become the world's most profitable smartphone platform.

Without any instructions from Apple, or official documentation for the iPhone hardware, a disparate band of hardcore programmers tasked themselves not simply with designing apps for the iPhone, but with reverse-engineering the iPhone's operating system so that these apps would run. Although today's iOS programmers have hundreds of pages of Apple manuals and a vast online community to help them create software, these early pioneers were operating blindly, using experience and guesswork to decipher exactly how the iPhone's software had been put together. When the iPhone first launched it wasn't even possible to boot up the device without authorization from AT&T, let alone install software. The hackers would have their work cut out for them.

THE BOY GENIUS

The challenge to unlock the iPhone caught the eye of George Francis Hotz — known online as Geohot — an 18-year-old electronics prodigy from Hackensack, New Jersey. Hotz had grown up in the homebrew hacking community and was fanatical about electronics, particularly robots. Hotz recalls that he had even dismantled an Apple II out of curiosity when he was around five years old.

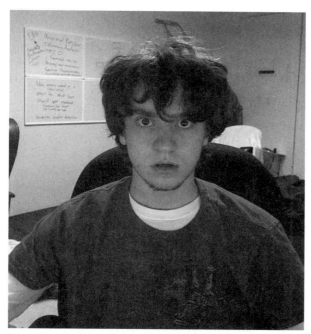

George Francis Hotz, or Geohot, was the young hacker who laid claim to figuring out a way around the iPhone's restrictions.

SOURCE: Reproduced with permission of George Francis Hotz © 2011 George Francis Hotz.

Answering machines, vacuum cleaners and television remotes were rarely safe around Hotz. He could not resist the urge to disassemble and tinker with their electronic innards. For years before the iPhone's launch he had been building and entering his homemade creations into science fairs. In 2004, aged just 14, Hotz had entered his project, "The Mapping Robot" into the Intel International Science and Engineering Fair, winning a Regional Award of Merit for "young technical and gifted students," and scoring him an interview with Larry King. This was a small taste of the media coverage that would come to dominate Hotz's later life; public attention he would eagerly embrace.

A year later, Hotz entered his robot "The Googler" into the same fair, this time reaching the finals of the competition. This robot was followed by a string of bizarre and technically imaginative projects, including one called "Neuropilot" in which Hotz attached sensors to his head to monitor the electroencephalography (EEG) signals emitted by his brain.

Neuropilot was a home-built sub-$8,000 device that allowed Hotz to investigate his brain using home-built hardware together with free software from the OpenEEG project. The OpenEEG group is a collective that allows hobbyists to get involved in neurofeedback or EEG biofeedback training. This neurofeedback process that Hotz explored is described on OpenEEG's website as "a generic mental training method which makes the trainee consciously aware of the general activity in the brain [and] shows great potential for improving many mental capabilities and exploring consciousness."

It was in this same spirit of inquisitiveness and invention that, in the summer of 2007, Hotz set his sights on the ultimate prize: to unlock the iPhone. This would be one of the first steps in allowing the device to accept apps designed outside Apple.

In retrospect, it's tempting to frame Hotz's motivations as ideological. When he later hacked the PlayStation 3, he claimed "information wants to be free." But with the iPhone the decision was less philosophical, and rather more practical: Hotz was on a T-Mobile phone contract, but the iPhone only allowed AT&T subscribers. Hotz simply wanted to use the iPhone with his existing contract. As he puts it, "the [T-Mobile] termination fees were insane" so he did what any other self-respecting hacker would and decided to crack open the iPhone. This was a task that would take Hotz more than 500 hours of work over his summer vacation in 2007.

"There were nights I would go to sleep at nine in the morning and then wake up at four in the afternoon," Hotz told *Marketplace*. The process of unlocking the iPhone was arduous and complex, but as he got further into the project he found he could not stop.

"If it was just about using it with T-Mobile I wouldn't have done it," Hotz said later in a live interview with CNBC. "But this was fun. I became obsessed with unlocking this phone."

His solution to cracking the iPhone was like something straight out of a school science fair project. It involved wires, soldering irons, and customized software. When news of his success hit the media, Hotz was invited to physically dismantle the iPhone in front of millions of Americans watching the evening news and demonstrate his hack. To a world that has largely forgotten how to change the oil on their cars, let alone reverse-engineer a printed circuit board (PCB), this was an extraordinary sight. Holtz showed a bemused newscaster how he shorted two contacts on the iPhone PCB to enter the iPhone's test mode and then used customized software to trick the device into accepting SIM cards from any network. Hotz had created the ultimate science fair project, a project far more popular than any robot. In the process, he had become the most famous hacker in America.

> *"I would love to have a talk right now with Steve Jobs," Hotz announced to the live CNBC audience. "Man-to-man, that's the kind I like."*

Steve didn't call.

Hotz's plan now was to put the unlocked iPhone up for auction on eBay, but within hours pranksters had driven the price up to $99 million, forcing the auction to be abandoned. Hotz quickly changed tack, offering the phone on his blog. The posting was picked up on by Terry Daidone, co-founder of CertiCell, a mobile-phone repair company based in Kentucky. Daidone arranged a now-legendary deal with Hotz. In exchange for handing over the world's first unlocked iPhone, the young hacker would be given Daidone's Nissan 350Z — a high performance sports car — and three brand-new 8GB iPhones. The final part of the deal was the offer of a consulting job for Hotz, so that CertiCell could learn how to unlock other iPhones and train its staff.

"We do not have any plans on the table right now to commercialize Mr. Hotz' discovery," Daidone told reporters. "However, we are keenly interested in having Mr. Hotz assist our engineers."

THE HACKER ARMY GROWS

Hotz continued to work on hacks for the iPhone, but now he had competition. A bunch of clever software hacks to open up the iPhone appeared on the scene. Any iPhone owner with an interest in tech back in 2007 would have familiar with a host of peculiar utilities, including PwnageTool, BootNeuter, and Yellosn0w. This host of bizarrely named programs were coded and released for free by equally bizarrely named hacker-groups. There was iPhoneSimFree — a hacker team that demonstrated that Hotz's hack could be done without physically opening the iPhone. There was also the influential iPhone DevTeam, a loose international team of hackers that described itself as "a group of people who work together over IRC from various parts of the world... a completely self-managing, self-regulating and member-funded organization."

Another interesting character was 37 year-old Italian hacker, Piergiorgio Zambrini — known to most of the community simply as Zibri . He would become, for some, Geohot's nemesis. Zambrini created an application that automated many of the steps in the unlocking process, popularizing the technique for a less savvy audience.

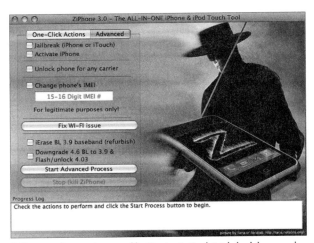

ZiPhone, a software suite created by Piergiorgio Zambrini, helped the general public unlock their iPhones.

SOURCE: Reproduced with permission of Piergiorgio Zambrini © 2011 Piergiorgio Zambrini.

Depending on who you ask today, Zambrini is either one of the greatest hackers of his generation, or a misanthrope who stood on the shoulder's of Hotz's work. Some members of the hacker community were outraged by Zambrini's popular ZiPhone software, but they were equally distressed by Hotz's television appearances. They felt the Hotz's openness with the press violated their "strict hacker code" and broke the cover of a private group that "would more than likely not recognize each other if [they] walked past one another on the street."

*The iPhone DevTeam took to referring to Hotz disparagingly as,
"the self appointed media front man for last year's iPhone hacks"
and claimed that he "couldn't abide by rules" — the hacker code.
They also claimed that Hotz had led a "media circus" and asked
him to leave the hacker community.*

Hotz's repeated appearances on television didn't sit well with the anti-capitalist ideologies of the iPhone DevTeam, although they appeared blind to the obvious irony. They were all developing software for the world's socioeconomic elite — who else could afford the first iPhone?

APPS INVADE BY STEALTH

In-fighting broke out between various hacker enclaves, but progress on developing for the iPhone continued throughout the summer of 2007. It culminated in the achievement of a hacker named RipDev, who finally completed the iPhone puzzle, launching a piece of software called installer. app. This was the crucial link between third-party apps and the iPhone. Installer.app let the owners of jail-broken iPhones install software on their devices. Used together with Cydia or Icy (two homebrew predecessors to the official App Store), it was now possible to browse a library of apps and install them on your phone with a few taps of the finger.

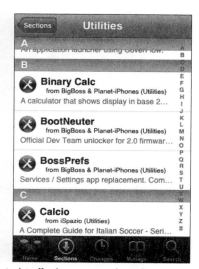

Cydia was the iPhone's underground app store before Apple's official version stepped onto the scene.

SOURCE: Reproduced with permission of Jay Freeman © 2011 SaurikIT.

By the fall of 2007, users who had jail-broken their iPhone — using the suite of hacker's tools — now had access to a fully functioning App Store with hundreds of games and utilities available to download for free. The strange thing was, Apple hadn't built this App Store, or agreed to any of it.

By the time of the App Store's official launch, the jail-break community had been installing and using apps for almost six months. It had all been made possible by a hardcore set of programmers who just could not wait for Apple to get around to allowing apps on the iPhone. They'd set about figuring out how to make software without the company's help.

When the official App Store opened in 2008, many of the programmers whose apps appeared on the new store had already been developing them for a year, honing their skills in the wild west of the jail-break community. Now these programmers could go legit and unleash their creations on the credit-card wielding iTunes-loving masses. It was going to be one hell of a party.

Jail-breaking in action: The process was complex for inexperienced users, but it meant access to apps months before Apple sanctioned them.

THE BEDROOM PROGRAMMER AWAKES

In the heady months of late 2007, there was a sense that something peculiar was about to happen to the computer-software scene.

The garage-programming scene had been stagnating for years. Traditional computer game budgets had escalated into the millions and many indie developers were effectively shut out of the mainstream console market. Sony's PlayStation and the Nintendo Wii were no place for a bedroom programmer. The price of entry alone was off-putting.

The cost of the development kit for the PlayStation was a minimum of $10,250 and a similar kit for the Wii cost anywhere from $2000 to $10,000. Even then an indie software developer would have to convince an existing publisher to distribute their title.

The only viable alternative for a small team was to distribute PC or Macintosh software over the Internet. But this tactic smacked programmers square in the face a seemingly unsolvable problem: Customers were unwilling to make the thousands of credit card payments necessary to recoup development costs on a modest software project. There was, sadly, no centralized, easy way to buy and sell software over the Internet.

The newspaper and magazine industry had clearly demonstrated that consumers weren't keen on paying small fees (micro-payments) for access to content over the Internet — the publishing industry was floundering — and newspaper marketing teams were far better equipped than any home-programmer. What hope did the independent developer have?

Not only did indie developers have no easy means of advertising their software, but they also had no method of collecting credit card payments that didn't involve the customer filling out a bespoke form for each transaction. The software industry was a hodgepodge of disconnected websites and incompatible payment mechanisms. Consumers didn't have the patience, or the confidence, to enter their credit details in every esoteric form they came across. But the problem was much bigger even than this. The simple fact was that the public had made a collective judgment that the Internet was "free." In a post-Napster world, it was almost impossible to get people to pay for anything online.

This was a landscape where a title's only hope of real success was to be bundled with PCs, or physically sold on the shelves of Best Buy.

THE ITUNES SUPREMACY

Apple realized that the solution to this tangle had been staring the company in the face: Why not take the same mechanisms used to sell songs on the hugely successful iTunes and use them to sell software for the iPhone? The idea was attractive enough for investors to jump in right at the start — years before *Angry Birds* was so much as a sketch on a diner napkin.

To coincide with the announcement of the App Store, Silicon Valley venture capitalists Kleiner Perkins Caufield & Beyers launched an "iFund" — a $100 million stash available to anyone who, in KPC&B's opinion, could demonstrate "market-changing ideas and products that extend the revolutionary new iPhone and iPod touch platform." While the world was yet to see any tangible evidence that money could be made from Apple's mobile application store, there was already optimism in the industry. There was a belief that Apple's infallible string of successes — from iMac to iPod to iPhone — meant the company would not struggle to attract consumers to its new App Store.

TRISM

While the venture capitalists danced their grim fandango of cash, the future Appillionaires sat crouched over their Macs, eagerly installing the official Software Development Kit (SDK), a free download from Apple that allowed anyone to try their hand at programming for the iPhone. Across the world, thousands of programmers began to explore what Apple's new toolkit had to offer. By September 2008, just two months after the launch of the App Store, something bizarre happened. Rather than Disney or Nintendo, or any one of the established software companies striking it rich on the App Store, it was a lone individual who emerged as the first poster boy of the iPhone platform — a 29-year-old programmer from San Francisco named Steve Demeter.

Demeter came from inauspicious beginnings: He had been a software engineer for ATMs. But after attending an iPhone conference the year before the launch of the App Store, he saw potential in Apple's new platform and began work on an app.

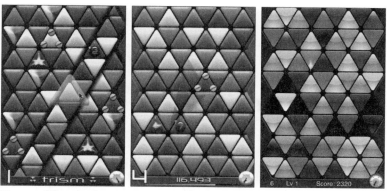

Trism, one of the earliest-known success stories on the iPhone.

SOURCE: Reproduced with permission of Steve Demeter © 2011 Demiforce LLC.

Demeter was one of several programmers whose app actually predates the existence of the official Apple App Store. Demeter first released his game to the jail-break community through the Cydia store.

When Demeter's app, *Trism,* was later released on the official App Store in 2008 it earned him more than a quarter of a million dollars in just two months. The game was sold at $5 (a price that would be unsustainable a year later as the race to 99¢ began). *Trism* was downloaded by thousands of iPhone owners but Demeter had spent very little money on creating the game — paying just $500 to a friend who had produced the graphics — yet the return was astronomical. This, the remarkable difference between the cost of developing the app and the amount it made on the App Store, would become a running theme in the Appillionaire story and provide an irresist-ible enticement to hundreds of other developers dreaming of riches.

Coding in the Dark

Trism began life as a project on the iPhone well before the official App Store opened. Demeter worked with the unofficial and unsupported tools that George Francis Hotz and the other iPhone hackers had developed over the summer of 2007.

> *Demeter would later describe this first attempt as "a bit of a kludge . . . I really had to go back to my roots as a low-level hacker in order to be patient enough with a system like this."*

Demeter's talent was in his ability to navigate both the maze-like complexities of the undocumented iPhone OS and yet to have the artistic sensibilities to produce a genuinely enjoyable gaming experience. Like many successful app designers who would follow him, Demeter was that rarest of creatures — an artist and an engineer.

When Demeter created the first *Trism* game he didn't have access to a Mac — not that this necessarily hindered him; there were no official development tools on the Mac back then either.

In a triumph of inventiveness, *Trism* was hacked together on a PC using an open source toolkit called the GNU Compiler Collection, together with a UNIX-like interface for Microsoft Windows called Cygwin. These two tools allowed the earliest indie programmers of the iPhone to develop apps without help from Apple. Neither tool was designed expressly for the task, but it all worked — just about. Developers the world over were running similar creaking, leaky hacked-together Frankenstein's-monster iPhone development kits. These were acts of engineering brilliance and technical finesse borne out of desperation to be the first to create apps for Apple's device.

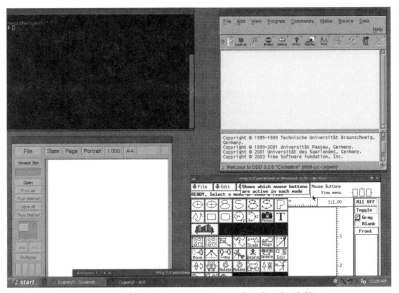

Early iPhone programmers were forced to resort to esoteric Windows-based tools like Cygwin.

SOURCE: Reproduced with permission of Cygnus Solutions © 2011 Red Hat.

For a non-programmer, the extent of Demeter's ingenuity is difficult to put in perspective, but imagine trying to compose a complex musical piece on a piano, in a pitch-black room, without being able to hear the notes you're playing. Programming for the iPhone before Apple's official SDK was a similar experience.

The tools Demeter used were so crude that the system was not even able to tell him accurately when and where an error had occurred in the code he was working on.

Programmers can find it hard enough to solve a problem when they know where the problem is located in the code. But to watch your app fail to work and to simply know only that somewhere, vaguely among these thousands of lines of numbers and symbols, there is a problem; that is an enormous test of patience and skill.

Trism Goes to GDC

Demeter worked around the clock to get *Trism* ready for the Game Developers Conference (GDC) in San Francisco. The GDC is the biggest gathering of game developers on earth and Demeter was hopeful that a games company at the conference would snap up his work and publish it.

On February the 18th, 2008, Demeter arrived at the Game Developers Conference. It was a crisp, clear day in San Francisco and the sun was shining as Demeter walked up to Howard Street to the Moscone West Center. He entered the building and stepped into the fray of developers, graphic designers, and engineers eager to figure out what the next big thing in the games industry would be. In his pocket, Demeter carried an iPhone with *Trism* installed on it. He went from publisher to publisher, showing off what would later become, for a while, one of the most popular games in the world. He showed these games publishers how *Trism* reacted to the orientation of the iPhone — using the accelerometer. He walked them through the gameplay and clever sequencing of shapes and colors.

How did these companies react — these kings and queens of the videogames world — did they offer him a job, or negotiate a licensing deal? No.

They told Demeter that his game was worthless to them because there was no way it would make money.

Selling *Trism* His Own Way

It was then that Demeter made a decision that would change the public perception of what it was to be a programmer forever. It was also a decision that would give hope to hundreds of other programmers who would later tread the same path. Demeter would publish the game himself and promote it through YouTube.

"I sent the link to 50 friends and contacts, thinking it'd have maybe 1,000 views or so," Demeter later explained to *Knitware*. "What happened though blew away my expectations. Within four days, it was up to 100,000 views!"

Within just two months of Apple's official App Store opening, Demeter had made over $250,000 from his game, and the money kept rolling in.

For the first time in history, the work of an individual designer-craftsperson was being sold and promoted through the retail arm of a globally powerful multinational that never met the artist in question. This unlikely combination of David working with Goliath meant that a programmer like Demeter, working in his bedroom in San Francisco could, for first time, make millions of dollars without leaving the house.

> As one indie developer, Peter Pashley, creator of the iPhone app *Aftermath*, later explained it to me, "It was the first time that a distribution channel existed for a single creative to distribute their work to tens of millions of people. If you're a musician that never really happens — unless you have a label. If you're an author that rarely happens — unless you have a publisher. People are actively looking for apps all the time and, if you make something good, it has the potential to spread like wildfire. Books and CDs never had that."

With *Trism,* indie programmers now had their major success story on the iPhone. The age of the Appillionaire had begun.

SUMMARY

Here's a roundup of the important points covered in this chapter:

- The iPhone didn't technically have any apps at all when it first launched. Apple bundled a few software programs that it later came to be understood were "apps," but third parties could not write software for the device

- A group of determined hackers led a community effort to "jail break" the iPhone and allow users to install software on the iPhone without Apple's blessing.

- By the time the official App Store had launched, many developers had been working on games for months and there were hundreds of apps available for underground app stores like Cydia.

- *Trism* was one of the earliest known success stories of the official Apple App Store. The developer behind *Trism*, Steve Demeter, had originally written the app without any help from Apple whatsoever. At the time he first programmed the app, there were no official Apple tools available for developers on the iPhone platform. His achievement was an impressive feat of ingenuity and determination that would inspire the app scene for years to follow.

THE
APPILLIONAIRES

6

DOODLE JUMP

IN THE SUMMER of 1991, Croatia was at war. The Republic of Serbia in the former Yugoslavia had invaded the newly declared state. In the shadow of the Croatian War of Independence, two young brothers from Croatia — Igor and Marko Pusenjak — were crouched in the glow of their ZX Spectrum 48k. Pixels blazed late into the night as the two children imagined the possibilities for a game they were designing. Igor took a pencil and a notepad, sketching out character designs and levels, while Marco experimented with the capabilities of the Spectrum. The brothers taught themselves BASIC — a simplified programming language designed to help first-timers learn their way around a computer — but Marko alone would go on to learn Assembler, a notoriously difficult low-level programming language — a delicate, precise way to tell the computer what to do *quickly*. Only the bravest programmers go near it.

The brothers' game design used Tom and Jerry as characters. It was based on an entertainment format already established on the ZX Spectrum — similar to the games that the brothers liked at the time — a combination of arcade and adventure. In Igor and Marko's sketches for the game, the player would guide a character. The character would have to find an object, pick it up, and then work out how the object could be used to progress the storyline. In one episode that Marko recalls, the player would find a key to open a door. Behind the door they'd find a chest. Inside the chest were some rings and these rings were then useful for the next task. It was a tried-and-tested format, but not many children were designing the levels.

"That was our first computer and we were taking it way beyond just playing games on it," Igor says. "Back in those days [software] was sold on tapes through stores. You couldn't self-publish. Being in Croatia at the time, it was even more difficult to do anything — rather than being in England where all the publishers were. That was an obstacle."

CROATIAN DREAMS

Today we live in an era of broadband Internet, USB drives, and iTunes, so it's hard to imagine the problems facing Igor and Marko in getting their game published back in the early 90s. It was a near-impossible task for an experienced programmer, let alone a young boy.

This was a curious era in which many games were distributed on cassette tape and loading software was a laborious process. Setting up a computer to play a game like *Donkey Kong* or *Chuckie Egg* was a feat roughly on par with complex surgery and was done by watching the odometer on the computer's cassette deck and then listening carefully — as a doctor might hold his ear to a patient's chest — for that telltale sign that one chunk of code had ended and another one would soon begin. Then you instructed the computer to "listen" to the tape and load the game — a feat that could take it as long as half an hour and had a thrilling habit of failing half-way.

Into this landscape, Igor and Marko sketched and programmed. By the end of the summer the brothers had their game mapped out in intricate detail — it filled many pages of the notebook. But soon summer was over and school had begun. Dreams of publishing their game faded with the heat and it was quickly forgotten among the new friendships and excitement of the fall term.

A REUNION

Igor would eventually graduate from high school and enroll in an American college, while Marko remained in Croatia. For three years of college, Igor was separated from Marko by thousands of miles and the roar of the Atlantic Ocean. But, back in Croatia, the brothers' notepad sat quietly in a drawer, its pages filled with a young boy's videogame dreams. Waiting.

While Igor studied overseas, Marko absorbed himself in programming jobs in Croatia, experimenting with Macromedia Director, a multimedia authoring platform similar to Adobe Flash. He had an idea that he'd like to create educational game for children, but his paid work got in the way and Marko never produced the kind of software he and his brother had sketched out over that summer in Croatia. But, in the spring of 2008, Marko got a phone call from Igor. This call would unrecognizably change both of their lives forever. Igor wanted to create a game for the iPhone.

Igor Pusenjak, co-creator of *Doodle Jump*.

SOURCE: Reproduced with permission of Igor and Marko Pusenjak © 2011 Igor and Marko Pusenjak.

THE EARLY DAYS

"The idea of the two of us working together on a project had been around [for years]," recalls Igor. "We were both working with Cold Fusion programming. We were constantly trying to figure out ways to do things together on some kind of project."

"[So I said], 'Okay, the App Store is opening: Marko let's do something together!' It was all done by email. Marko was doing all the programming; I was doing all the graphics and the art. I would work here in the U.S., and he would wake up [in Croatia] and everything was ready for him [because of the time difference]. Then when I woke up I could answer his questions."

Don't Talk About the iPhone SDK

Unlike programmers today, Marko did not have access to much documentation explaining how software should be built for the iPhone. Apple had placed the iPhone SDK (Software Development Kit) under a legally enforced contract of secrecy, known in the industry as an NDA (non-disclosure agreement). This meant that programmers were not allowed to discuss their tips and tricks for developing iPhone apps openly on the Internet. Today there are hundreds of forums where developers can help each other out with iPhone programming problems, but Igor and Marko built their first app almost completely alone — their only real source of information being the guides provided by Apple.

With the launch of the App Store weeks away, the brothers began a frenzy of coding and design to get their first app completed in time. Rival developers already had a head start in using Apple's Xcode software because it resembled the programming suite used to create application for desktop Macintosh computer — but Igor and Marko were out of luck. Neither of them knew how to program for the Mac or the iPhone, so they set about figuring out how the system worked. Initially, the two brothers started programming together, but it soon became clear that Marko was faster and better at coding that Igor. Marko raced through Objective C manuals (the language used by the iPhone), but information on the brand new iPhone was limited.

Igor and Marko realized early on that their first app would have to be something simple — there wasn't time to reach a high level of competency with iPhone programming — it was then that the pair struck on an idea.

BUBBLEWRAP

"We decided to create *Bubblewrap* because we thought it would be simple to do," recalls Igor. "Well, Marco thought it would be easy to program, but it actually took weeks."

Bubblewrap was an app that simulated the popping of plastic air bubbles in the packaging material of the same name. The iPhone screen showed the user a photo of a sheet of bubble wrap and they were free to pop away: a strangely pleasurable experience that psychologists would have a field day explaining.

Bubblewrap, Igor and Marko Pusenjak's first attempt at an iPhone app.
SOURCE: Reproduced with permission of Igor and Marko Pusenjak
© 2011 Igor and Marko Pusenjak.

"It was simple and silly enough that we thought we could do it and people would be willing to pay 99 cents," says Igor. "That was always the intent for us. You would just press a button [to download the app] just like iTunes; that was the [powerful] model that existed. We also thought that it was silly enough that some journalists would pick up on it."

With the App Store yet to open, the brothers had no evidence that their idea might be a commercial hit. But Igor remembers that he had a kind of hunch that something special was about to happen. He often found himself thinking back to Steve Job's speech at the launch of the iPhone in which Jobs stated Apple's goal of capturing just one percent of the cell phone market. Despite sounding like a tiny figure, this would amount to 10 million iPhones sold. This led Igor to a smart extrapolation: If Apple could make money selling just 1 percent of the cell phones on the market, perhaps Igor and his brother could make money selling to just 1 percent of iPhone owners.

> *"The moment they opened the App Store, they had ten million devices out and ten million credit cards on file," remembers Igor. "But I had no idea it would be so huge, not even close. I've been an Apple fan boy for a very long time; I love everything Apple. It was an opportunity.*

[I thought:] let's see what we can do; it's a new market. Apple is taking care of distribution. If we can just get one percent of that market, it's incredible. When you look at the numbers, that's huge."

The brothers never dabbled on the early, unofficial app store created by the jail-breakers (see Chapter 2), but began work on *Bubblewrap* shortly after the announcement of Apple's official store. But then, after weeks of frantic work, disaster struck. Twice.

DISASTER STRIKES TWICE

Igor and Marko submitted *Bubblewrap* to Apple in time for the launch of the App Store and it was approved for sale, but their developer agreement — the contract between every programmer and Apple Inc. — had been delayed. This meant that their app would not appear on the store's launch day. It seemed like all their hard work had been for nothing. The App Store launched, but the brothers' app was nowhere to be seen. Worse still, because the most recently approved apps appeared at the top of the page in iTunes, when *Bubblewrap* finally appeared it was shunted down the page by more recently approved apps, pushing it to the fourth screen — somewhere few people would find it.

Igor remembers, at the time, the App Store was a very different place from what it would later become.

"There were only 500 apps and you could actually — and I did, on the first day — look at everything that was out there," he says. "[*Bubblewrap* was] not at the top, but the first day we sold 50 or 60 copies, which honestly I thought was amazing."

"We didn't have the aspiration of creating hundreds of thousands of dollars, or millions, or have any wild dreams about it. We thought let's get some income that will help us pay for fun things, like going out, and some extra. I [looked at the sales figures for *Bubblewrap* and] thought, that's cool, but imagine how much more we would have made at the top."

As if being hidden on the fourth page of apps wasn't obstacle enough for the pair, there was worse to come. The day before *Bubblewrap* finally became available for sale, a rival developer came out with a competing *Bubblewrap* app for the same price. Initially this was just an unfortunate coincidence, but a few days later that rival developer made a decision that would undermine Igor and Marko's app: He made his competing app free.

"It was in the days when everyone was bitching [and saying:] 'apps should all be free'," remembers Igor. "And this guy got scared and made his app free. He was then the number one bubble app."

Determined to keep fighting, the brothers responded to the move with characteristic optimism. "[We thought:] 'so what'?'" Igor remembers. "The first version [of our *Bubblewrap* app] was simple and selling well. So we thought, 'let's add some more features.' We added more details and submitted the update."

KEEP ON UPDATING

"Back in those days the updates would go straight back to the top of the charts. We launched the first update and it was like, boom! Two hundred copies sold. We thought 'Wow! This is really great!" We thought let's seriously continue working on this. The more content we give people for the update the more they love it — but it also goes back to the top of the charts. This was our approach [from then on]."

IF AT FIRST YOU DON'T SUCCEED . . .

The next app idea the brothers came up with was a Japanese language tutorial in the form of a *Kanji* flash-cards app (Kanji are the Chinese symbols that are used in written Japanese). It was — as I get the impression with so many of the brothers' choices — a decision driven entirely by emotion. They decided to make a Kanji tutorial simply because Marko wanted to learn Japanese. In a modern business landscape choked by MBA-graduate hack philosophies, it's refreshing to learn that almost everything that led to Igor and Marko becoming multi-millionaires was driven by whim. Amazingly, the middle step in their journey to one of the greatest business success stories of the decade was Marko deciding he'd quite like to learn Kanji.

Igor and Marko Pusenjak made this *Kanji* flash-cards app. The launch was a disaster.

SOURCE: Reproduced with permission of Igor and Marko Pusenjak
© 2011 Igor and Marko Pusenjak.

"I was learning the Japanese language for a few years," explains Marko. "So after *Bubblewrap* I thought I could make some flash-card applications. The initial idea was, Let's make it for myself to help me to learn Japanese faster and to try to learn programming for the iPhone. I put lots of the [Kanji symbols] in, and the app looked like it could be useful to other people."

The brothers launched *Kanji* on the App Store, expecting huge success for their new invention. But then disaster struck. Again.

"Just like with *Bubblewrap* — two days before our Kanji app went live — someone else came out with a Japanese Kanji flash-card app," remembers

Igor. "We were devastated, I mean seriously devastated. With *Bubblewrap* it wasn't such an original idea, but with *Kanji*, we thought, 'okay what are the chances in the world?' Right? So we had a little bit of a crisis especially because with *Bubblewrap* the idea was always that it would be 99-cent app because it was silly, cheap, you know, and it just made sense. [But] *Kanji* was going to be about five dollars and," Igor continues, visibly saddened even all these year later, "there were four different levels of *Kanji*!"

"There are four levels of the Japanese language proficiency test," Marko explains. "So in the beginning I put in only the first level with basic *Kanji*. But the guy [whose app was launched] a day before us actually included all four levels, which is 2,000 Kanjis!"

"The idea at first was to sell each level at five dollars," says Igor. "So we were going to sell each level. And then this guy comes out with all four levels for three dollars total! We had no choice but to price ours at 99 cents and then we started working on the next app."

Igor laughs, realizing the ridiculousness of it all.

Both brothers have an innate cheerfulness to them. It seems to have served them well in brushing off the mixed success of their early apps. It's also endearing that the two most successful iPhone developers in the world still feel a kind of sadness that their early *Kanji* app failed to become a hit.

TIC TAC TOE

"So, the [next app we built] after that was again something very simple," says Igor. "It [was based on an idea that] already existed, but there was [a special look and feel to it]. Not necessarily the birth of the *Doodle Jump* style — I think I can trace that back earlier — but it was the first of our apps that used a notebook-type of style and was just basically a tic-tac-toe game."

Again, the brothers picked a simple idea and chose to execute it well. Marko remembers that he chose the *Tic Tac Toe* project because it would help him learn more programming on the iPhone — he was still grappling with how to make the device do what he wanted. The game launched quietly on the App Store and saw moderate success.

"It went pretty well actually," says Igor. "Especially in the beginning. I think someone already had a *Tic Tac Toe* game out when we came out. There were certainly others and, right now, there are tons of others. But it was something people liked. It looked nice — at least I thought so — and again, it was 99 cents. Not a lot of money to spend on something where you have some fun."

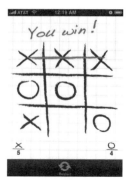

Building on the experience gained
from making their previous apps, Igor
and Marko Pusenjak made this game
of *Tic Tac Toe*. It sold moderately well
but was not a hit.

SOURCE: Reproduced with permission
of Igor and Marko Pusenjak
© 2011 Igor and Marko Pusenjak.

Although the pair was already seeing small profits from their first few apps, there was no clear direction and *Doodle Jump* was yet to be imagined. For their next project, Igor suggested creating an app that would test airplane pilots looking to get their licenses. Igor was a great fan of flying and, with typical haphazard delight, simply 'liking' an idea was all the justification needed for the project to go ahead. So they set about creating flight-preparation apps alongside the existing *Kanji* apps.

> *"[We found inspiration in] the things that were close to home,"*
> *says Igor. "Marko with Japanese; me with flying. We were trying*
> *to grab a niche."*

Once the pilot training app was launched — to achieve relatively unremarkable sales — the brothers made the first in a series of choices that would guide them to the highest ranks of Appillionaire. They decided they would make a game, but it wasn't *Doodle Jump* — although that's where it would lead — it was an app called *Eat Bunny Eat*.

EAT BUNNY EAT

"One of the things Marko did with Macromedia Director was a catching game," remembers Igor. "And I was trying to figure out how to create some fun graphics [for that game mechanism]. So, *Eat Bunny Eat* was our first original game on the iPhone and surprisingly — well not surprisingly — it was actually fun and addictive when you played it."

Eat Bunny Eat. Some of the design ideas in this title would be carried over to the smash-hit game *Doodle Jump.*

SOURCE: Reproduced with permission of Igor and Marko Pusenjak © 2011 Igor and Marko Pusenjak.

"One of the best comments we got was from a group in England. They were playing it in the pub, passing the phone over and screaming eat, bunny, eat! I imagined how that scene looked. Getting comments from the people playing your game is, I think, the most rewarding thing ever. We were touching someone far away, someone that we don't really know, and they were reacting in such an incredible way. That was really something that pushed us to go on and on."

A HAND-BUILT LOOK AND FEEL

This was to be the beginning of the brothers' adventure. They had progressed from the basic design of *Bubblewrap* all the way to through to the detailed gameplay of *Eat Bunny Eat* in that first summer of the App Store — between July, when the App Store opened, and August. Although they didn't realize it at the time, the pair was carving out what Igor calls "a children's niche." Today it might seem a given that making children's apps is big business, but back then many programmers wondered if the iPhone would find itself remote and inaccessible to a younger generation. Children's apps were not an obvious choice for developers.

> *"The big question back then was: Would parents give a $600 device to their kids to play with?" remembers Igor. "And, you know, we didn't know. But then everyone we observed playing our games who had kids, [realized] they can go to a restaurant, give [the kids] this iPhone, and they play Tic Tac Toe for two hours and are quiet."*

Igor's simple but important observation would change everything, and he was right. Many parents were in fact only too happy to give their children Apple's expensive slab of electronics and glass, no matter how much it cost. This was because, in return, they would be rewarded by the most priceless gift a child can give to parents: Silence.

"So we figured we were onto something there," says Igor. "But part of the problem with the kids niche is that — it is a niche. So the strategy [was], Let's see if we can design something that appeals to everyone: to both kids and grown ups. Our sensibility naturally leans towards a kids style — I think that's where a lot of the design and look and feel come from."

It was around this time that the brothers started hearing about the first few big success stories, like that of *Trism* — the first big advertised success story on the iPhone. But, despite the gold rush erupting around him in the media,

Igor remained firmly grounded in the reality of the store. There would be, he felt, no quick fortune to be made here. The plan for their next app, *Doodle Jump*, was not to create an overnight success, but simply to create one more app that would help the brothers learn more about programming and design so that they could improve their skills for future releases.

> *"We were not thinking, you know: 'Oh, it will be easy to make a hit game' and it wasn't necessarily a plan," says Igor. "[There was no] strategy to make a hit. It was more like: 'Let's make some solid, fun games that people will want to buy and let's make 10 . . . 20 . . . 30 of them and it will all add up. The Trism story didn't make us think: 'This guy made tons of money, we can do that too!' No, it didn't happen in that way."*

"The idea from the beginning was never 'Let's make tons of money on this.' It was, 'let's do something together and have some fun and see what happens.' Not to say we weren't interested in making money; for sure we were, but that wasn't the primary goal. Not in the way [some] investors and speculators invested $50,000 into finding a development team and creating and app that only made $10,000. From the beginning, our investment in money was very low. It was mainly time."

THE HERITAGE OF *DOODLE JUMP*

In designing *Doodle Jump*, the brothers were careful not to make the same mistakes that they saw others making across the industry. Newspapers and blogs were keen to promote the mythology of the wealthy independent app developer stumbling on easy riches, and it was easy to get carried away in the hype: over-investing and ruining yourself in the belief that success was inevitable. But Igor and Marko had already witnessed the heartless truth of the App Store: You never knew what would happen — it would be reckless to predict success for any one app, and therefore reckless to pour money into a single idea. The brothers also had one interesting advantage over many other app developers — an advantage that is shared by more than one outlandishly successful developer: They were family.

The bond between Igor and Marko is more than a quirky aside to their story. Igor believes it was central to their partnership and the very reason *Doodle Jump* exists.

"There's an issue of trust," explains Igor. "You trust your friend, but you trust your brother even more than a friend. You know them, more than you know some developer that you have contracted out for the job. The one thing that I find most problematic in outsourcing is communication. If you can't communicate clearly with the other party, it's a problem. [Marko and I] knew each other; we spoke the same language; we knew how to communicate."

Eat Bunny Eat was a more successful launch than any of their previous apps, selling enough copies to keep Igor and Marko in business while they hatched new app ideas. The brothers came to the logical conclusion that they should make a sequel to *Eat Bunny Eat*, but, once again, the process of invention for Igor and Marko did not involve marketing projections and brainstorming meetings. *Doodle Jump* was conceived in a world set apart from corporate bureaucracy. Instead, it evolved from a simple question that the brothers put to each other back in 2008: "What else do bunnies do?"

"They eat carrots," Igor remembers deciding with Marko. "But they also jump. So we thought, 'let's make a game where a bunny's jumping, and picking up carrots or something.'"

From this simple idea, a fortune was grown.

DOODLE JUMP IS BORN

Marko began working on a game engine for a new game where a jumping bunny gobbled down carrots as he scaled platforms on the screen. While he built and programmed the jump mechanism, Igor was supposed to do be doing graphics. But things weren't going well for Igor.

"I was trying to use bunny graphics," recalls Igor. "The grass things — all that — and it just didn't look right."

Igor struggled to produce graphics he was happy with — his perfectionism seemed to outdo him at every turn. Like any artist who gives in completely to the inner voice, the voice that whispers that the artist's work is not yet good enough, Igor found himself in a rut, paralyzed, and frustrated. Days passed in a fruitless introspection until Marko finally called Igor and told him, "I need something to put in, give me anything."

"So I did these basic sketches as placeholders," remembers Igor "So Marko could continue programming. They were basic placeholder images . . . [But then] we kind of started liking [the placeholder sketches]; it was fun and different."

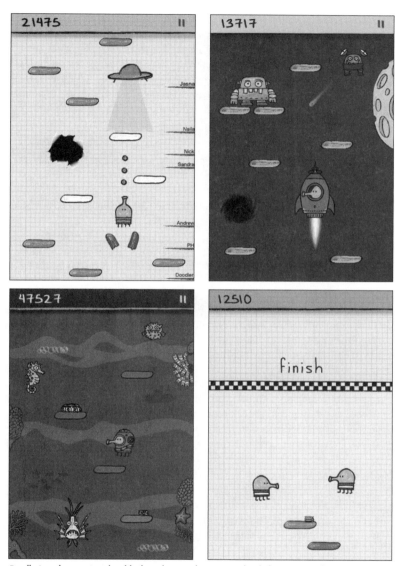

Doodle Jump has a unique hand-built quality to it that resonated with the gaming audience. Set against the stark lines of the iPhone, the game has a warm, heartfelt look.

SOURCE: Reproduced with permission of Igor and Marko Pusenjak © 2011 Igor and Marko Pusenjak.

By some peculiar quirk of the universe, the fact that Igor couldn't seem to make suitable graphics for *Doodle Jump*, led to one of the most distinctive game aesthetics on the iPhone: its distinctive sketchy, hand-drawn look. Because Igor sketched the graphics for *Doodle Jump* in a crude back-of-a-napkin style, the brothers realized that the game had began to take on a unique character that more technically sophisticated games seemed to lack. Because the graphics for *Doodle Jump* were never created with the intention of actually using them in the finished game, they had an unusual warmth and playfulness. Where rival games had money and style, *Doodle Jump* had heart and soul.

THE ORIGINS OF THE SKETCHED AESTHETIC

Just as Steve Jobs traces the success of desktop publishing on the Mac back to time he spent in a calligraphy class, Igor has a theory that the *Doodle Jump* aesthetic can be traced back to his grad school.

"For one of my favorite projects in graduate school we were supposed to make a visual interpretation of James Joyce's 'Finnegan's Wake'," Igor recalls. "If you've ever encountered it, you'll know how crazy that piece is. So, I just did crazy sketchy hand-drawing things and which were not particularly awesome compared to some of the people in my class, who were amazing illustrators and artists. But, to my surprise, everyone loved it. [They were] looking at it saying, 'this is different; this is great.' [That is why I reconsidered the original *Doodle Jump* graphics] and thought, 'Hmm . . . Okay, there is some merit to it.'"

In a traditional games studio, you can imagine the art department having a fit over the decision to abandon polished graphics and opt for the casual scribblings that were meant to be placeholders for the real graphics. But this studio only had two employees — two brothers — and both were sold on the idea of sticking with the happy accident that had resulted in the now famous *Doodle Jump* look and feel.

"We liked the style. It was different from things that were out there and we really liked the way it was starting to look," says Igor. "We decided to start with that and maybe build the bunny game [we were originally thinking about] later."

ADDICTIVE QUALITIES

As anyone who has played *Doodle Jump* knows, the graphics give the game a special look, but it's the gameplay that really sets it apart from the hundreds of other games competing in the App Store. So what is Marko's secret; how did he make *Doodle Jump* so irresistibly addictive?

"I am a kind of perfectionist," explains Marko. "I try when I program to make the animations [smooth]; I always try to make a game that runs perfectly."

"For example, you can [choose to] make things the easy way, but performance-wise, I put a lot of time into making the details perfect. Because of that, the game runs really perfectly smooth. The first main engine on *Doodle Jump* wasn't that complicated; I think I did it in three weeks. Without the graphics — without everything — just the main game engine. We didn't have graphics at the beginning, we didn't know what the graphics would look like, so I used the placeholders Igor sent me and I was just programming and testing and seeing how it feels until it felt… perfect."

"And this is the big difference between working with your brother rather than hiring someone," says Igor. "When you work for yourself, your goal is to make it perfect, when you're working for someone, your goal is to just get it done. So Marko wasn't like, 'Okay, this is working, I'm done,' and then sending it to someone else and asking them, 'Are you okay with it?' and them saying, 'No, this is not good, make it better.'"

Because the brothers were able to avoid the tiresome back-and-forth that tends to happen with hired developers, *Doodle Jump* was built quickly and, more importantly, with a supernatural attention to detail. Igor remembers one particular moment that illustrated the lengths Marko would go to in an effort to make the game run immaculately.

"When you look at [*Doodle Jump*], and look at the helicopter we have falling off. [Marko] spent three or four days just on perfecting that. He asked me 'Can you see the difference?' and I'm like, 'I can't,' and he said, 'but I can see it.' These are the sorts of things that you don't notice because they are so perfect, but have been a big part of the success of the game. You take it for granted that everything is running smoothly and it becomes invisible. But that is what makes a huge difference. When you don't see any issues."

Igor's idea that perfection is invisible reminds me of an adage that film editors have always believed. If a film is edited well, the audience won't notice it was edited well, because they won't notice the editing. The same goes for acting, and any number of other creative pursuits. As the artist becomes more proficient, she looks more effortless in her work, and the mechanisms that underlie the work become all the more concealed. Igor is right: perfection is often invisible. Of course, video games struggle to find themselves admitted to galleries or museums, but it's interesting to consider Igor and Marko as two of the most popular, and commercially successful, artists of their generation.

THE COMPETITION GETS TOUGH

Marko worked on the *Doodle Jump* game mechanism, and Igor made tweaks to the hand-drawn graphics he had created. Slowly, *Doodle Jump* began to take shape. But things were changing on the App Store scene, and the brothers were increasingly uncertain that there would be a place for a small indie game like theirs.

"In the very beginning you could basically put anything on the App Store and it would sell, just because there wasn't that much on it," Igor remembers. "[But] by Christmas 2009, the competition started to heat up because the *Trism* story was out — people were buying apps and all the bigger companies were now interested."

Igor remembers one very technically advanced and polished app called *The Chocolate Frenzy* that was particularly frightening because it implied a new corporate direction for the App Store.

"When [*The Chocolate Frenzy*] came out I was like: 'Oh my god, we are done!' [I thought] here is no way we can compete with studios that have [3D artists and professional animators]. We were two people; we didn't have money or investors. We weren't even looking for money or investors, and we couldn't pay 3D artists to make super-fancy crazy graphics. And I thought, 'Okay, we're in trouble now because there is no way we can compete with these guys.'"

The Chocolate Frenzy made Igor and Marko suspect that the iPhone games industry was getting too sophisticated for indie programmers to stand a chance.

SOURCE: Copyright Digital Chocolate, Inc.

In the face of a corporate invasion of the App Store, Igor took solace in the revival of simpler games. Both brothers still believed that a well-thought-out indie game design could beat a big-budget studio game. There was historical precedent for this theory. Alexey Pajitnov had created *Tetris* single-handedly while working at the Soviet Academy of Sciences. It went on to sell hundreds of millions of copies, becoming one of the most popular games ever created. Unfortunately it was years before Pajitnov saw any money from the game — due to the peculiarities of the political system under which it was made — but it did demonstrate the idea that while you could throw thousands of dollars at a studio-built game, sometimes all it takes is a lone individual with a great concept.

"The biggest inspiration for me was the Nintendo Wii," says Igor. "It really took a step back from graphics in favor of fun gameplay. And that was the thinking behind *Doodle Jump* for me. [I realized that apps don't] have to use some crazy 3D realistic graphics. It's about the fun gameplay and graphics that are fun and different in a way of their own."

"So [we stopped] trying to compete with everyone else [and instead we] tried to carve out our own space."

DOODLE JUMP FLOPS

Determined to build on the minor success of *Eat Bunny Eat*, the brothers completed the design of *Doodle Jump* and set it loose on the App Store. So how did one of the world's most successful iPhone games fare during its first outing on the store? It flopped.

Massively.

"I think *Doodle Jump* was probably the worst launch day of any of our apps," says Igor. "We were not sleeping at night — looking for comments on the App Store, because that's usually an indication that people are downloading it." Strangely, Igor couldn't find any comments on the *Doodle Jump* page. Apple doesn't release download figures until the day after a sale has occurred.

"We looked at the numbers the next day," says Igor. "We'd sold 35 copies."

"With some apps you get excited because you think they're fun, and then you launch them and then no one buys them and then you realize they're really not fun — you realize it. But with this one [we were convinced that] people will buy it right away, and tell everyone they bought it, and it will sell like hot cakes and," Igor can barely contain his disbelief even today, "It was really fun."

Igor and Marko looked at the low sales and then at the game again. They played *Doodle Jump* and became increasingly convinced that something had gone strangely awry.

"This is fun; there is something to this," Igor told Marko. They both agreed that it was time to do some "old fashioned PR" and actively sell the app to journalists and influential websites. "I sat down and wrote an email to every single blog, everyone and anyone who was writing about iOS games," Igor recalls.

"About a week later we actually got *Touch Arcade* — which is the biggest iOS gaming blog — to write about [*Doodle Jump*], and we thought: 'Now we're set; now it will sell and be a hit,' but that didn't help much either. We were again puzzled. What is going on?"

The brothers struggled to diagnose the problem. There was even a discussion about whether *Doodle Jump* would do better in a new category in the App Store. "Does this go into entertainment, or is it a game?" Igor wondered. They debated which was the best category for it. At one point *Doodle Jump* was hovering around number 90 in entertainment, a moment when Igor remembers being most incensed by the public's lack of interest in *Doodle Jump*. At the time, there was an app called Mirror — it was effectively a joke app that turned the iPhone screen black, causing it to become slightly reflective, but no more reflective than when it was switched off. The app was 99 cents and people were buying it because they weren't reading the description, thinking it was an actual mirror. Mirror was ranking above *Doodle Jump*, around number 75 in the charts.

"I thought, screw this!" remembers Igor. "*Doodle Jump* is not better than Mirror?"

It was difficult for the brothers not to become disheartened in the face of such absurdity, but they continued working on an update to *Doodle Jump*, determined to prove its value to an uncaring world. The game's initial failure in the market led to some serious thought about how to make an already addictive game mechanism all the more appealing.

TWEAKING THE GAME FOR SUCCESS

"One of the things that was the focus of my graduate school was this interaction between physical and virtual worlds," says Igor. "From the beginning, I was telling Marko we should integrate something that interacts between everyone who is playing the game. Of course, I like to overcomplicate things and create headaches for Marko to program."

Igor laughs.

"[I suggested to Marko that] when Doodle falls to the bottom [of the screen], maybe he appears on someone else's screen randomly — something super complicated."

As predicted, Marko thought the idea of Doodle jumping between gamers' screens would be a programming nightmare, but he liked the concept of interaction between different gamers and some kind of communal experience for the players.

"Why don't we put little markers on the screen to show how far everyone got?" Marko told Igor. "You see the markers and the names next to the markers, and you see how far [up the *Doodle Jump* world] everyone got to."

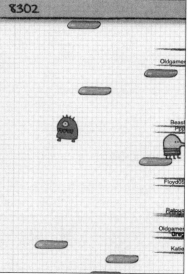

Doodle Jump includes a unique high-score system, whereby the progress makers of various players are displayed during the gameplay itself.

The pair agreed. And so did Apple — shortly after the brothers updated their game with progress markers, Apple featured *Doodle Jump* in a promotional spot on iTunes. But when this first wave of publicity hit, Igor was — rather dramatically — in a tent in the middle of the Sahara desert with no Internet access and absolutely no idea that *Doodle Jump* had exploded into the App Store charts. And while Igor slept under a starry desert sky, Marko was freaking out thousands of miles away in Tokyo. He had travelled there to continue learning Japanese, enrolling at a language school and working on improving *Doodle Jump* from his MacBook Pro. For weeks, Marko had been careening between cafés and anywhere else he could glean a WiFi signal.

"I remember walking around Tokyo," says Marko, "and trying to find WiFi that was free around the city just to check what's our position on the top charts. When we got featured it was moving up like crazy, every few minutes a few places. Up and up! It was fantastic, really it was a fantastic feeling."

Doodle Jump hit the top 100 apps and continued to climb. Over in the Sahara, Igor had no idea what was happening. He had decided to tour Morocco to relax, and get away from *Doodle* for a while. Little did he know that Doodle was about to find him.

"I got to this place in Fez," says Igor. "There was an Internet connection and I had hundreds of emails from Marko. My favorite one was: Now? NOW? Now you choose to go to the desert without an Internet connection?"

"I realized now we had to push [*Doodle Jump*] to websites, send more PR around, and hope to get coverage in *Gizmodo* and some of the other blogs. It was really back to work."

A GLIMPSE OF SUCCESS

Igor returned from the Sahara and watched Doodle rise up through the charts, first into the top 50, then into the top 25. The brothers had the feeling that this was as high as the game could climb. They had sipped from the Holy Grail; Apple had featured their app and the world had woken up to *Doodle Jump*. Just as it seemed like the game was unstoppable, the three-week Apple promotion was over and *Doodle Jump* sunk inexorably down through the charts. Igor was shocked.

"We were like, 'Oh, gosh that didn't work, why is that?'"

By June 2008, *Doodle Jump* was still in the top 100 games, but then fell out of the top 100 apps altogether. But the brothers still kept working on updates, adding new game elements and other details that customers had said they liked. "We were trying all kinds of things," says Marko. "The advertising didn't work, you couldn't really buy your way into the charts, so one of the things that came into my mind were, okay, let's try something different." But no matter what the brothers tried, it seemed that they just couldn't maintain *Doodle Jump*'s position in the charts. So determined not to give in, they decided to work on a sequel: *Doodle Jump 2*.

DOODLE JUMP 2 IS BORN

The brothers thought it would be fun to take a popular character from another iPhone game and place it in the *Doodle Jump* world. The game *Pocket God* was extremely popular at the time — and still is. Without any particular marketing plan, the brothers decided to put a *Pocket God* character into *Doodle Jump* as an "Easter egg" (programmer slang for a hidden bonus in an app that rewards the user with an amusing treat). Igor got in contact with Dave Castelnuovo. He was in luck, because Castelnuovo had not only heard of *Doodle Jump*, he was a big fan. He thought Igor's idea was wonderful.

"That's definitely something that helped a lot because they pushed the game to their fans," Igor says. "It generated some press because it was the first time on the App Store that you had this crossover of characters from one game to the other; it was interesting; it was something different."

Then, around the middle of July 2009, for no clear or explicable reason, *Doodle Jump* began to climb through the charts again. Igor was amazed.

"Suddenly *Doodle Jump* was heading up the charts and that was without any specific promotion from Apple, or promotion from anything that would be short-lived, but through the organic [process of] friends telling their friends."

Doodle Jump ended up peaking at number four in August. It lingered in the top five from August to February. Then, one crisp winter's morning, it finally reached number one in the U.S. App Store.

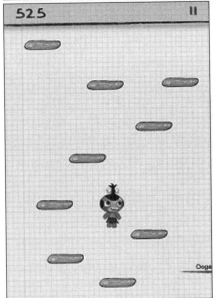

Doodle Jump characters appeared in other game franchises as a clever cross-promotion scheme.

SOURCE: Reproduced with permission of Igor and Marko Pusenjak
© 2011 Igor and Marko Pusenjak.

"Finally one day I woke up and it was in the first place," says Marko. "I couldn't believe it. It was a really special feeling. I remember taking a camera and just taking pictures of the iPhone and *Doodle Jump* in first place. I was thinking, 'It will not stay there,' so I just wanted to take pictures. [I thought], 'Okay, it's number one; we made it.'"

"It's like every time you check again, you're afraid it's not going to be number one," says Igor. "It was amazing… but there's always this… I guess I would call it fear: 'It's not going to last forever.' Apps go up and then they fall and we have quite a few apps that sell, you know, one or two copies a day. We know how bad it can get."

When *Doodle Jump* finally hit the top spot in the charts, Igor was in Mexico in a town that had no electricity and no Internet connection. It was becoming something of a traditional that he would be in a remote location as soon as Marko needed him urgently. Igor thinks he was probably the last one to find out that *Doodle Jump* had hit number one, "It seems like all the major points in *Doodle Jump*'s success I am somewhere without the Internet."

"We definitely celebrated," remembers Marko. "[*Doodle Jump* spent] a long time at number two. I don't remember exactly which app was in the first place . . . I remember waking up every morning and checking: is [*Doodle Jump*] in first place? Is it in first place? I think it was maybe 10 days it was in second place. Number two is fantastic, but number one is number one!"

"It's like every time you check again, you're afraid it's not going to be number one. It was amazing," says Marko.

Most games that reach the number one spot in the App Store peak quickly and then fall off. But for all the time it took *Doodle Jump* to reach number one, the brothers were rewarded by a long stay at the top of the charts.

Buoyed by this incredible success, the brothers began to theme *Doodle Jump* around major holidays. In October they released a Halloween-themed *Doodle Jump*, and then in December a special Christmas edition. It was the latter that really tipped the fortunes of the pair, propelling *Doodle Jump* to number 3 over the critical holiday season and cementing the app as one of the iPhone's most memorable titles. It also attracted the attention of the Venture Capitalist's flapping tentacles.

"I don't remember exactly when it started; I would say it started gradually. [Investors] starting giving us calls for all kinds of things. I think it was after [*Doodle Jump*] was number one."

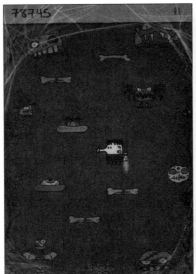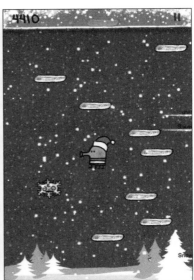

Doodle Jump is often redesigned to celebrate major holiday events — creating another wave of excitement.

SOURCE: Reproduced with permission of Igor and Marko Pusenjak © 2011 Igor and Marko Pusenjak.

Igor and Marko turned down offers to buy out their small — albeit it now fabulously wealthy — company, valuing what they had built and refusing to give into the temptation to let corporate giants buy into the success they could not seem to achieve for themselves.

> *"Independence has been great and it has also cost us," says Igor. "But I think for us that [independence is] more important than trying to grow super fast."*

"I guess my life has become more fun. One of the things that I enjoy is interacting with people, and through *Doodle Jump*'s success I have been able to do that — through going to conferences and talking to other developers, talking to the press, all of that. It's also really, really exciting to be working on something that's your baby, basically, to the point where our mom jokes that *Doodle* is her grandson."

When *Doodle Jump* became a global success, the brothers were working all day building updates for the app and can't remember any big celebration.

HOW *DOODLE JUMP* CHANGED THEIR LIVES

"I didn't have time to enjoy it, to celebrate, it's just work, work, work. But the freedom I have now [is hugely rewarding]; it's like we can do whatever we want with *Doodle Jump!*" says Marko.

Given all the press hype surrounding the Appillionaires, it's interesting to note that, despite selling over ten million copies of *Doodle Jump*, Igor and Marko still spend their days much as they did in the years leading up to the app's success.

"It's one of those things that's weird. Everyone is expecting [me to say], 'Yeah I bought two Ferraris and a jet'," says Igor. "But in reality you don't have the time to do that. Life is definitely more relaxed in terms of not having so much to worry about: will you make the rent this month. Or, can you afford dinner out? But, I think the real changes will probably [become clear] in a few years when we're actually deciding how to continue this, when you stop having the pressure. This is an amazing opportunity right now and we have to keep going 24 hours a day to keep it alive. I don't know if that ever stops. If you look at Steve Jobs, or you look at [Mark] Zuckerberg [the creator of Facebook] — these people who build something out of nothing — it keeps going. But at some point you treat yourself, I guess."

Igor is aware that *Doodle Jump*'s success has been used by the mass media to set-dress a popular fantasy of easy riches on the App Store. He's quick to point out that even without *Doodle Jump*, both brothers were making enough money to survive.

"With the apps that we had [before *Doodle Jump*], both of us could make a very decent living doing what we love without anyone telling us what to do. [There are] developers who have not necessarily reached number one, but are putting a lot of work into what they do… they're actually making some nice money right now."

> *"I think persistence is the most important thing; people think that they will create an app and they will make millions right away on it and that's it. But it doesn't happen overnight. For us, it didn't start with the App Store; it started when we were 12. Everything that we have done so far led up to it."*

It's true that Igor and his brother began this journey back in Croatia decades earlier. They didn't read a magazine article about iPhone app designers and decide to throw $10,000 on to the App Store roulette table. The fact that these two brothers were able to take care of the art, sound, marketing, programming, and promotion ideas for the app is a testament to indie development. It's hard not to find their story inspirational.

It was because of the seemingly unrelated things each brother had done before — Igor's strange and wild drawings of James Joyce's poetry in grad school; Marko's love of the Japanese language — that led the pair to a point where *Doodle Jump* sprung from some deep unplumbable well of human imagination and into reality. Igor had worked in publishing and advertising, he'd studied graphic design and programming — all kinds of things that helped him reach a point where success became possible. Marko, similarly, has programmed most of his life, and explored game possibilities for much of his career.

> *"I think there has never, in all history, been such a tremendous opportunity like Apple has created with the App Store," says Igor. "Whereby having knowledge of programming — of interaction — you can create something that can be distributed to so many people in the entire world without having to put a big investment up front. Literally, all you need is a hundred bucks a year for the developer license, a laptop, and knowledge. [In exchange], you have world-wide distribution; so I think it's tremendous for independence and for people who have been inventing games their entire lives."*

"[Previously] there was never really an opportunity to create something on your own and be your own publisher and distributor. You always had to be attached to a publisher. But now you can do it."

So what does Igor make of the mythology surrounding the Appillionaires?

"You know media loves to be media, and loves to make big headlines out of everything. There has definitely been a gold rush mentality among a lot of people who have heard the success stories and thought, 'Oh yeah! That will be easy!', but it's very difficult, especially now, and you have to know what you're doing. Above all, you have to be persistent, just like with anything. It's not the App Store only; it's anything in life. Persistence is what counts, and not everyone is cut out to do that."

Perhaps the most overt sign of success is when the former leaders of an industry you come to dominate can do no more than imitate your product.

That moment came for Igor and Marko when a knock-off of their app, *Pac'N-Jump*, was created by the famous development studio, Namco.

"It's pretty incredible that a company like that is taking inspiration from us," Igor says, laughing. "It's a game like *Doodle Jump*, only with *Pacman*."

Pac'N-Jump pays homage to the world of *Doodle Jump*.

SOURCE: Reproduced with permission of Namco © 2011 Namco.

Igor pauses to consider his words, "I guess that's flattering?"

It's historical.

SUMMARY

Here's a roundup of the important points covered in this chapter:

- Igor and Marko started young. They both had a serious interest in computers and programming from childhood. This put them at a huge advantage over many other iPhone programmers, who decide to take up programming purely for profit. Coding was in these guys' bones.

- Both brothers collected a lot of life experience prior to launching an iPhone app. One of the reasons *Doodle Jump* looks like it does is because of Igor's training in the liberal arts. This is not the sort of progression you could predict. If there's something to learn from the brother's career paths it's this: Do what you love. Vocational-based training can be great, but often it's the obscure, unexpected connections drawn from a broader understanding of art and history that inspire the real breakthroughs in life. *Doodle Jump* has as much to do with the literature of James Joyce as it does with Objective C.

- The brothers experienced many setbacks before striking it rich with *Doodle Jump*. Theirs is a story of persistence in the face of failure. Don't expect your first iPhone app to be a hit. Just like Igor and Marko, you will have to work toward eventual success.

- Working in a family team lends a special quality to a project, as does working with someone in a different time zone. Igor and Marko took advantage of the fact they could program from anywhere in the world, and used this as an opportunity to travel and explore. If you're looking for an escape, but want to continue working, designing apps for the iPhone is a job that requires no office and very little infrastructure.

- *Doodle Jump* was initially a flop, but the brothers had the intelligence and skills of self-evaluation to realize that they should not give up on the title. Knowing when to stop is just as important as knowing when to battle through the difficult times. Have faith in your app ideas but, equally, don't discount the possibility that it may be time to move on to another one.

- The most successful iPhone developers, like the *Doodle Jump* brothers, are more interested in quality and achievement than financial success. Money is the reward for their hard work, but becoming fixated on the idea of a potential fortune in the future is extremely stifling to creative thought. Make brilliance your objective, not wealth.

7

HARBOR MASTER

IF YOU TAKE a guided tour of the *Harbor Master* team's "World Head-quarters," the "first executive suite" turns out to be a kitchen table. The "deluxe executive suite" looks suspiciously like a bedroom. And, as Natalia Luckynova and Keith Shepherd show you around their workspace, the truth quickly becomes obvious: This is in fact their apartment — this husband-and-wife team who created *Harbor Master* work from home on a near-zero budget. Yet their company, Imangi Studios, is one of the most successful iPhone publishers on the planet. Until recently it only had two employees, both of which still sleep just a few feet from where they work.

Imangi Studios has a YouTube video tour of their office that you can watch online. It's an irreverent parody of the self-important marketing dross of traditional video games publishers. In a very real sense, Luckynova and Shepherd have embarrassed the multinational developers, outshining this competition despite working out of a tiny apartment in Washington D.C. It would be hard to find a more powerful example of how the bedroom app developer has risen to fame and fortune thanks to the uniquely meritocratic landscape of the App Store.

ROMANCING THE APP

Luckynova and Shepherd met and married while working for the healthcare industry developing web applications — neither had any proven experience in making games, although they both held degrees in Computer Science. As a kid, Shepherd had entertained the idea of working for the games industry, but when he left college he found himself in the midst of the dotcom boom and was swept away in his enthusiasm for web development and, for years, his idea of making games was forgotten.

Like Shepherd, Luckynova had also become trapped in the drudgery of building web applications for the healthcare industry.

"I never really knew what I wanted to do; growing up I was always a generalist," Luckynova remembers. "I liked music and working with Keith, but we were both frustrated with our jobs and working for somebody else all the time."

The pair sat in an office, coding mundane systems for a computer network they cared little about. Through marriage they had formed a team that would eventually come to dominate the app scene, but back then neither of them would have guessed it — for now they were code monkeys in an anonymous machine. The days at work dragged on.

AN ESCAPE FROM BOREDOM

Then, one day, Shepherd snapped.

"I was getting really frustrated with my job, so I quit," says Shepherd. "I had the intention of starting a new company. I'd had an iPhone since the first day it came out, and thought it was a neat piece of tech — I was tinkering around with it in my spare time and then I put together this little puzzle called *Imangi*."

Meanwhile, Luckynova kept working her job at the healthcare company.

"I decided I would keep my job and support us," says Luckynova. " This would give Keith the freedom to figure out which direction we were going to go. He came up with the idea for a game called *Imangi* — it was a really cool puzzle — it seemed like an amazing job to be able to make games. I helped him out and supported him and encouraged him to go in that direction."

Keith Shepherd's first game, *Imangi.*

SOURCE: Reproduced with permission of Imangi Studios © 2011 Keith Shepherd.

The App Store was yet to officially open and neither Luckynova nor Shepherd were aware of the illicit "jailbreak" app scene — the unofficial channel that enterprising programmers had set up to distribute iPhone software. Shepherd designed his puzzle game without any idea of just how big the app market would eventually become.

"We didn't hear any success stories, because the App Store didn't exist when we started," says Luckynova. "We came up with an early game idea and went with it on a whim."

Shepherd had liked tinkering around and making his own small games, but prior to the App Store there wasn't a good way to make a living doing that.

"The only option at the time — as a small one or two person team — was to make Flash games for the web," says Shepherd. "I never went that route, but, knowing folks who have done Flash games and little games for portals on the web, it's extremely hard to make any kind of money."

> *"It's only the really big players — the guys who own these conglomerates — who made money on the web, not the small developer."*

"We thought, okay, let's do this," says Luckynova. "We'll start a business. We'd make games."

"It was funny, because I remember thinking to myself before I launched *Imangi*: 'I've spent about a month making the thing; if I make a thousand dollars in a month, that would be really cool. I could then make a lot of little games and make a living out of it.'"

A MONTH OF CONFUSION

Shepherd would soon discover that he had wildly underestimated just how popular the couple's games would become. In the beginning they had no idea of the potential reach of games on the App Store. In the weeks before the store opened, there was no clear data on just how many people would end up downloading apps. Today, a developer will receive a sales report every 24 hours — letting them know how many copies of their app have been sold in the last day. But back when Luckynova and Shepherd launched *Imangi*, Apple provided developers with sales reports just once a month. The tension was unbearable.

"We went an entire month in confusion," says Shepherd.

"Nobody had any idea how many apps they were selling," says Luckynova. "We were totally in the dark."

Luckynova decided she would pass the time by creating a series of increasingly wild and speculative mathematical models. She would use these models to blindly predict sales.

"I basically assumed that a week into it we were probably millionaires, according to the various graphs and charts I made," says Luckynova. "But other days I thought maybe we'd made zero." She laughs. "It was ridiculous."

> *"When we got our first sales report I thought we might make a thousand dollars in the first year of selling Imangi," remembers Shepherd. "But we made quite a bit more than that just in the first month. That was the moment I realized, 'Wow. Okay. I'm going to focus all my efforts on making games for the App Store. There really is an opportunity here.'"*

BUILDING ON SUCCESS

The couple continued making smaller apps, which found modest success on the store, but there was no stand-out hit. There was enough money trickling in for Shepherd to feel secure in having quit his job, but battling it out in trench warfare with thousands of other small games was a tough business.

Summer came around. In the warm weather, Luckynova and Shepherd would often take sailing trips — sailing had always been one of their favorite hobbies. One afternoon on the water, a thought formed in Shepherd's mind. As he watched the boats coming and going, docking and steering around each other in the glare of the afternoon, he had an idea.

HARBOR MASTER IS BORN

"So I was out on the water in my little boat," says Shepherd. "At the time there was a line-drawing mechanic that I'd been thinking about on the iPhone. It was a really revolutionary thing as far as control mechanisms go for iPhone games [you draw a line with your finger and objects or characters in the game follow the line]. We were playing around with some different ideas for using a line drawing mechanic in a game. Out on the boat that day, I realized that there was a perfect match between this mechanic and boating. We imagined this little game with boats, where you had cargo on them, and you were dropping the cargo off and leaving the dock. Using the line-drawing mechanic."

It was this idea that would evolve to become the iPhone's smash-hit game *Harbor Master*.

Harbor Master would be Luckynova and Shepherd's fourth app. The couple always has a running list of ideas they want to work on — just little snippets of thoughts they think "might be cool." Every time they finish one project and move onto another, the couple consults the list, deciding which ideas they will quickly prototype and experiment with. Shepherd had added the idea for *Harbor Master* to this list of ideas and Luckynova agreed that it looked like something they should build into a demo to see where the idea would lead. Because Imangi is such a small company, the team chooses only to work on smaller projects, things that might take between two to four months to build from start to finish. Mostly casual games.

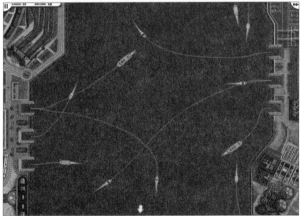

The smash hit app *Harbor Master*. The idea for the game idea came to Luckynova and Shepherd when they were out on a sailing trip.

SOURCE: Reproduced with permission of Imangi © 2011 Imangi.

The following spring, the couple was getting down to the water more often, sailing on their boat. They decided it was time to run with the game idea they had sketched out. In the end, *Harbor Master* was put together in just two months and launched shortly after the Apple WWDC (World Wide Developers Conference). It turned out to be the most impressive launch Imangi ever had.

"I think *Harbor Master* resonated with game players at the time," says Shepherd. "People were looking for more games using the line drawing mechanic. Plus, it was summer time and lots of people enjoy boating in the summer. We launched at a really good time and the game was featured by Apple. This was a really big deal."

Harbor Master was launched and it shot up the charts. Shepherd was stunned.

"It was amazing! The most success we'd ever had with any of our apps. We were really shocked. We beta tested — we had players play with the apps — so we knew we were onto something and people were really enjoying it, but it really blew away all of our expectations."

Luckynova could hardly believe what was happening.

"It was very emotional," she says. "I couldn't do anything except watch the charts for weeks. I was pretending to work but really I was looking at stats. It's like watching yourself win the lottery in real time. You see *Harbor Master* going up and up the charts. You're asking yourself: 'Is it going to hold that position?' There's an obsession to it."

"It just blew us away how well it was doing," says Shepherd. "On its way up, we were really relieved to watch it go — you never know how high it will go. You hope it will go to the top of the charts, but 99 percent of the time it doesn't. There's this nervous moment where you're trying not to get your hopes up, but at the same time you're very excited. When it starts to go down, that's when it starts to get depressing. It's only downhill from here. It's nerve-wracking."

A HIGH-SCORE EXPLOSION

It finally became obvious that the couple had hit the big money when the server running the *Harbor Master* high-scores "essentially exploded," says Shepherd.

"We were using a shared host [a web server shared between several users] and we got a call from our hosting company. They said, 'We've had to shut down your server because you were using 100 times your bandwidth.' All of a sudden we had to scramble to get a dedicated server to host our high-score leaderboards. It was a very frantic time for us when *Harbor Master* launched. We weren't really prepared for that."

"On the way up the charts, you're aware that this is a golden opportunity that happens very rarely," says Luckynova. "You're thinking: 'How can I take advantage of this? Do I make another update? Can I do more marketing? How can I make it stay up there longer?' You don't stop thinking about it and you get preoccupied with all these ideas about how to keep the app high in the charts. It's an exhausting feeling like that 24/7. Never in my wildest dreams did I think it would turn out as big as it became. We made our first games for fun. We didn't think that would even be something that we could devote all our resources to and form a company around. It was a very happy time for us."

MARRIED LIFE

"The amazing thing with the App Store is that it really lowered the barrier to entry," says Shepherd. "Small mom-and-pop shops can release little games that they made in their spare time and be able to reach this worldwide audience, without having to deal with all the intricacies of payment systems."

Luckynova had quit her job in healthcare and joined Shepherd full time by this point, helping out with coding and also composing all the music for their apps. I ask them if they found working as a husband-and-wife team a strange experience.

"It's funny," says Shepherd. "Whenever we tell people that we run a business together, you either see one of two expressions on their face. It's either utmost horror. They think: 'How can you work with your spouse, you must be at each other's throats all the time, I could never do it. I'd go crazy!' Other people think it's the coolest thing ever. It's neat that you get to spend so much more time with the one you love, working together on the same projects. Working as a family unit in the same company has challenges, but it's also, for us, an amazing thing. We both have skills that complement each other, so it makes every one of our projects better than it would have been if just one of us was working on it."

Luckynova agrees.

"I do realize that the only time we fight it is about work," she says. "Because I think we both get passionate when there are differences." But, she deadpans, "It's always fine and resolves itself when Keith admits that I'm right."

BIG PROFITS, SMALL TEAM

The couple has found that, from a lifestyle standpoint, the success of *Harbor Master* has improved their relationship immeasurably. Both Luckynova and Shepherd now have extremely flexible schedules, and can work from anywhere. Although the couple still spend most of their time working out of their apartment in Washington D.C., they've also spent time in various coffee shops across the city and travelling around the world. As Shepherd puts it, "if you want to take the day off in the middle of the week, we can do that. We're flexible as a family."

"It's really fun working together!" says Luckynova.

"It does really blur the boundaries between our life and our work, though," says Shepherd. "We spend a lot of time thinking about work outside the nine-to-five — a time when we're not supposed to be working. That can be a challenge. But working together as a family — I think the benefits of it really outweigh everything else."

The couple is amused by the apparent power and authority that success has brought them, but they're acutely aware that the App Store gives a false impression of the scale of their company. Shepherd has found that many customers assume that Imangi is a giant "faceless corporate machine" churning out apps. A company like EA or Sega.

> *"Sometime we get really goofy support emails," says Shepherd. "Some people made assumptions about the size of the company and the way we work, but really it was just the two of us — now three. We're a really small team and we care deeply about all of our apps. We often have way more on our plate that we have enough resources to accomplish."*

It's an interesting position for a team of bedroom developers to find themselves in. When a tiny group of developers finds global success on the App Store, the reaction from the public can be quite overwhelming. In the past, it would have been impossible for such a small number of people to sell a game to millions of customers, but Apple's bizarre marriage of garage developers to its fiercely powerful global distribution arm make the sales figures astronomical. The public then tends to assume that the companies behind successful apps must be giant organizations. Often they are just individuals with a keen mind and a good sense of what gamers want.

Luckynova and Shepherd are often bemused by people's perspectives of what a small app team might actually look like — one of the reasons why they have posted a video tour of their "World Headquarters" on YouTube.

"We just work out of our house," says Shepherd "We're a small team trying to make great apps."

Natalia Luckynova and Keith Shepherd,
the husband-and-wife team behind
the *Harbor Master* app.

SOURCE: Reproduced with permission of
Natalia Luckynova © 2011 Keith Shepherd.

GROWING THE TEAM

With the success of their apps, Imangi added an artist who works with them full-time — bringing the team to a magnificent total of three people. Despite having just one member of staff, Luckynova insists on taking attendance. It's a running joke based on their love of the television show "Flight of the Conchords" — the cult comedy where a two-person New Zealand band struggles to make it in New York City. In the show, the band's manager call the members into band meetings and insists on reading out their names, to which the band must respond out loud, allowing their manager to formally mark attendance despite it being painfully obvious that everyone is present.

"We take attendance as a joke," says Luckynova, "To make it more like real work. So we would actually get out of bed on time we would have morning meetings."

BEHIND THE SCENES

So, how does an app at Imangi Studios take shape? It depends on the project.

For most of their projects, Shepherd programs many days for 14 hours straight in what Luckynova affectionately calls "his coding cave." Luckynova's work will vary, depending on how involved she is in any particular project. She might also be coding on it full time, or she may be working on the music. Luckynova is also responsible for working on Imangi's older projects, making updates and maintaining the code. It depends on where the team's apps are in their lifecycle and, she says, "What I feel like doing that day."

Imangi is entirely self-sufficient. Luckynova and Shepherd do all the programming, music, sound effects, and game design from their one-bedroom apartment. They devise the story and the marketing behind their games too. The only thing they found lacking in their innate range of talents was graphic design. The solution was to hire a full-time artist, Kiril Tchangov.

Tchangov now does all the art in the Imangi games. Everything from the 2D character illustration to the backgrounds.

"He just does it all," says Luckynova. "From our marketing material to advertising on our website. 3D models, 2D models — all of that stuff — he helps us shape the environments and the vision — deciding how things are going to look."

Luckynova and Shepherd often meet people at industry gatherings and are asked what they doing in the tech scene. No sooner do they mention *Harbor Master* than the mood changes. Almost everyone seems to be a fan — the game is on millions of devices — and if the person they're talking to doesn't play, they always seem to know someone who does. Usually their spouse or children.

"It's mind-boggling," says Shepherd. "We never expected so many people would play something we created. It's always heartwarming to hear someone say they like your game and they played it; it makes you feel really good. But I can't really visualize it. I see the numbers that come in on sales reports and that has a very real impact, but I just…" Shepherd clearly struggles, even now, to fathom just how many millions of people have played their games.

"Some people spend so much time playing these games," he says. "We have stats on some of these games — the amount of human time people have spent playing *Harbor Master* can be measured in years, and years, and years. Some people have played hours of our game every day. It's really cool that we have been able to impact people's lives and provide entertainment."

Luckynova is also overwhelmed by the scale of their success on the iPhone and iPad.

"It gives you the feeling that everyone is a kid on the inside, playing these games," she says. "You walk around the city and everyone looks really serious. But in their spare time they're going off and playing this silly boat game and getting enjoyment out of it. It gives me this happy view that we all have joy and excitement on the inside. Maybe our games help people realize that and live those moments of joy. So that's really cool for me."

"I think things have changed for us," continues Luckynova. "When I quit my job we weren't sure that we were going to be able to do this for a while, so it was a big risk, and now we've had a successful app. We can work together out of our house, on whatever we want, our own projects; that's amazing. It's basically all I ever wanted: To have independence and be able to do what we want."

I ask them what they did to celebrate the success of *Harbor Master*.

"We always try to have a launch party," says Shepherd.

"We do?" asks Luckynova.

Clearly it was a fairly low-key event.

"We have a team dinner essentially," insists Shepherd. "It wasn't like we were having a party with lots of people and champagne; we just had a nice small dinner with the three of us. When we launched *Harbor Master* there was another person that helped us with the art, so there were four of us working on. Natalia and I full time, and two artists — contractors. The four of us went out after we launched *Harbor Master*. That was it."

So much for the Appillionaire lifestyle.

"You always feel weird celebrating an app success because you feel like you have to keep working to maintain it," explains Luckynova. "So it doesn't feel like, 'Oh! I've finally arrived, I've reached my potential.' Instead, you think: 'Okay, I've started, I've just started doing well.'"

"You don't want to jinx it," says Shepherd. "You know at some point it's going to go back down."

Luckynova and Shepherd feel that the independence and the creative freedom *Harbor Master* gave them has changed their lives in substantial but subtle ways. At their previous jobs in the programming industry they felt trapped and uninspired. Shepherd was particularly unenthused.

"I hated those jobs," he remembers. "I was never excited about anything that I was working on. They were jobs, they paid the bills. But working on *Harbor Master*, and creating Imangi, it doesn't feel like work anymore. It's what I would be doing if nobody were paying me for it. I really do enjoy making games and programming — it's fun doing it for the sake of doing. I feel incredibly lucky that now I get paid to do what I love."

SUMMARY

Here's a roundup of the important points covered in this chapter:

- Luckynova and Shepherd are, like many of the Appillionaires, a family unit. There is clearly something very special about working with someone you know and love. If you're looking to build an app business, it seems like the first place you should look for employees is in your own home.

- The couple built their business out of their apartment. This demonstrates great business sense. Don't get over-excited and spend too much on developing your app ideas: your biggest asset is your mind. Most app ideas don't need outside investment, and it's extremely risky to ask for it.

- The Imangi team designs apps they themselves love to play, and they took inspiration for *Harbor Master* from their sailing trips. Don't spend too much time thinking about app ideas; go out and live your life and the ideas will come to you naturally when the time is right.

- A good sense of humor is critical for indie app designers. There is so much that can go wrong and the market is incredibly risky. Luckynova also had the foresight to keep her regular job to support Shepherd until he had demonstrated that it would be possible for the couple to make a living independently. If your husband or wife is willing to do this so you can follow your app design dreams, you married the right person.

8 POCKET GOD

IF YOU PEERED through the window of the Castelnuovo house one afternoon in the fall of 1983 you may have seen a strange sight. You might have witnessed Dave Castelnuovo playing *Battlezone* on his Atari 2600. Behind him, on the sofa, you would see a representative from Atari. She is taking notes and watching the teenage boy intently.

Earlier in the same year, Atari had announced a *Battlezone* competition. The two gamers with the highest score would win a trip to the 1984 Summer Olympics in Los Angeles to take part in a grand playoff. The young Castelnuovo had read about the competition and had been practicing *Battlezone* for months, racking up the enormous top score of 999,990 — the maximum possible in the game. Today was the day of reckoning: Atari had sent out a team of investigators to double-check the scores submitted to *Atari Club Magazine*. Castelnuovo was on their list, one of the top ten *Battlezone* gamers.

The Internet was unheard of in the 80s and there was no way for the Atari 2600 to store the high scores the gamers had achieved. Instead, Castelnuovo had sent a photograph into the magazine to show his score. Now, to verify his achievement, Castelnuovo would have to play the game in front of the Atari representative and demonstrate his ability. While the Atari representative scribbled notes, the boy set up his videogame console. This was it. This was his chance to prove himself to Atari — at that time, king of videogame companies — and win a trip to the Olympics. There was just one problem: Castelnuovo had lied.

Castelnuovo couldn't play *Battlezone* at all.

Castelnuovo had hacked the system. He had fiddled with the loose power connector on his Atari console until it confused the game's loading system and gave him infinite lives. He had then taken a photo of his cooked score and mailed it to *Atari Club Magazine*. But now, under the stern gaze of the Atari representative, the boy could not bring himself to risk his deception being uncovered, so he loaded the game without tweaking the system's power-cable and played it straight, unhacked. His score was abysmal. The Atari representative looked at the boy for a moment, made her excuses, and left.

A BASIC START

Twenty years later Castelnuovo would be an Appillionaire and Atari would be bankrupt and largely forgotten. The boy had lost his chance to visit the Olympics, but it was the start of a lifelong love affair with videogames hardware and software engineering. What began with a simple hack on the Atari 2600 console would culminate in the iPhone game *Pocket God*, one of the App Store's most successful titles, with over 4.5 million copies sold worldwide and counting.

"I think to this day I could have pulled it off," remembers Castelnuovo. "[The Atari representative] was so clueless as to the games, that I could have done it," he insists. "Growing up, I've always been someone who wanted to mess with things and see how they worked."

Castelnuovo was lucky enough to find himself around computers as a young kid. This was rare at a time when the microprocessor revolution had only just begun.

"In 6th grade my teacher had a TRS-80 and he was the first person in the school to have computers in the classroom," says Castelnuovo. "It was and old machine and you had to boot up games from the cassette player. I started fooling around with that quite a bit, getting into it — learning how to change the scores. In those days a lot of the games were written in BASIC so it was really easy to get in and mess around with it."

The TRS-80 was an early computer made by Tandy Corporation and sold through Radio Shack. A theme began to emerge in Castelnuovo's approach: Again, his first instinct was to maximize his high scores without actually playing the games, but this soon matured into a desire to create his own software.

"I'd make it so you could get super high scores. Then the teacher let me take the computer home for vacation and I tried to write a role-playing game. I was a big fan of text-based adventures like *Zorg*. Adventure was the first kind of game I got started on. [I also played] some no-name games that I bought at Radio Shack. I learned BASIC and tried to build my own game. [But,] after that class we didn't have many computers in the classroom until college".

DROPPING OUT

After a break from computers, Castelnuovo enrolled in college to study Aerospace Engineering. Luck had it that in his junior year he was lodged in a room next door to a computer science major. Castelnuovo saw what his neighbor was doing on the computer and decided that "it seemed pretty easy".

Castelnuovo would make regular trips next door under the guise of drinking expeditions, but would often spend his time making "mouse cursors that looked like little bombs flying around the screen" and, later, 3D graphics.

"I got really interested in 3D graphics," says Castelnuovo. "*Wolfenstein 3D* had just come out. I did a lot of reading about assembly language — I was inspired by a guy named Michael Abrash. He was a genius. He used to work at Microsoft and he wrote a lot of the early optimization books for how to really get low-level with the [video graphics] hardware and figure out how to make it fly."

Not long after, Castelnuovo ended up dropping out of school — partially for financial reasons and partly because he'd lost enthusiasm for his course.

GETTING HIRED

He soon applied for a programmer's job in Orange County.

"I wasn't all that hire-worthy," says Castelnuovo. "I didn't have a degree or anything, didn't have a lot of experience. But I went in there and this guy said to me, 'Hey, this is Ringler Studios and it's a rocket ship blasting into the upper stratosphere and the last thing I need is for you to be my O-ring.' This was right after the Colombia Shuttle disaster blew up because of a faulty O-ring. It was a strange introduction."

Things got stranger still for Castelnuovo. He was then told that, although the lead programmer has recommended him, there were seven other candidates looking for the same job. Ringler told Castelnuovo bluntly that Ringler was a small company and the person who asked for the least amount of money would get the job.

"How much do you want?" the head of Ringler asked him.

"I completely freaked out. I thought, 'Oh crap! What do I ask for? $25,000? No that might be too high… 'I really want this job. So. I quoted him $20,000 a year and his eyes lit up like it was Christmas."

Castelnuovo hadn't really thought about the transaction properly. Ringler Studios accepted his offer and hired him. But Castelnuovo couldn't find rent that was cheap enough so he ended up sharing a house and "putting a ton of hours in." At one point, Castelnuovo's boss asked him if he owned a car "because he wanted me to sleep in it during the weekends so I could be close to the office."

Castelnuovo would regularly work through the night "until 5 or 6am," but it paid off. After month of working for Ringler he was made the sole programmer on a game called *Clay Fighter* for the Sega Genesis. On its release, the game became a hugely popular title.

Not bad work for a programmer on $20,000.

"It was just me and this other guy, and they threw a bunch of Japanese Sega manuals at us and said: Go for it! Make this game," remembers Castelnuovo. "It was kind of cool; I got my work ethic from that experience. Right now I do work pretty crazy hours pretty much seven days a week."

BUG-CATCHING AT SEGA

Castelnuovo quickly engrossed himself in programming for the genesis, working on *ESPN Football* and then *Clay Fighter*. Soon he was an experienced console programmer and made the move to Pacific Softscape, where he worked on a project called the Sega Channel. The Sega Channel was almost a weird precursor to the App Store. It was a hardware device that gamers could plug in between their Sega Genesis console and the cable TV network. It allowed users access to a rotating library of 40 games for $12 a month. Every month Sega would refresh the games on the network. It would be Castelnuovo's job to program the BIOS on the system (the code the box would use when first powered on).

Within a week of being at Pacific Softscape, Castelnuovo was sent to Atlanta to work on the new Sega Channel hardware. His placement in Atlanta was meant to last a week, but he quickly discovered that the Sega Channel hardware was horrifically flawed.

"I was sitting with all these engineers and they asked me to write a simple memory test so they can check their hardware. It came back false," remembers Castelnuovo. "They asked me, 'Are you sure there's no bug in your code?' Well, it was three lines long. I told them there was no bug in the code. A soldering mistake — a small error on the chip — made the memory test come back wrong. I ended up spending four months in Atlanta working with those engineers."

HARDWARE SECRETS

Unlike many Appillionaires, Castelnuovo's background is in hardware design as much as in software design. His experiences with the hardware at Sega were uniquely useful when it came to developing for the iPhone years later.

"It was interesting, getting into low-level hardware. It really forms the approach that I take today: Understanding the whole thing from start to finish. I think a lot of developers come in at too high a level and they don't have an understanding of how the hardware works, what the compiler is actually doing to your code: memory management."

> *"I can kind of see through to what the [iPhone programming language] is really doing," explains Castelnuovo. "You have an insight into things. When you say, 'render these 5,000 polygons,' you know what is the software is doing, and then what is the hardware actually doing. It gives you more of an idea — more of a space to innovate and come up with solutions on how to pull things off."*

When I speak to Castelnuovo, he has just finished his 39th update of *Pocket God*. The average app released around the time of the first *Pocket God* app would usually have only been updated once or twice. This is part of the game's appeal. But first — What is *Pocket God*?

HOW TO PLAY *GOD*

Pocket God is tricky to explain; you really have to play it to believe it, but here goes: You play a god in charge of an island of Oogs — tiny humanoid creatures. You can manipulate the little creatures, picking them up and dropping them in new locations, or changing the weather. Place an Oog in the water and it will drown — a strangely satisfying yet simultaneously cruel act. Initially the Oog characters were called pygmies, which sparked some controversy when Pacific islanders and anthropologists complained to Apple that *Pocket God* was exploitative.

"The game shows grass-skirted people next to an Easter Island statue. At the player's whim, they can be tossed through the air, fed to sharks, or set on fire," wrote the *New Zealand Herald* on April 30th, 2009.

The newspaper interviewed Canterbury University Lecturer Malakai Koloamatangi who protested: "You can't say this is anywhere but a Pacific island... If this was an African or a Jew or someone, people would be jumping up and down; but because Pacific Islanders are inconsequential, as it were, people are allowed to do it."

Surprised by this reaction to *Pocket God*, Castelnuovo contacted the Pacific Islanders and agreed to rename the characters in his game Oogs rather than pygmies, and to replace the Moai statue with that of an imaginary octopus god.

Pocket God allows you to play the role of a supreme deity, picking up small creatures and drowning them recklessly in the Pacific Ocean.

SOURCE: Reproduced with permission of Bolt Creative Inc. © 2011 Bolt Creative Inc.

CAPTURING THE MOMENT

The offence was unintentional, and the game quickly rose to become a favorite on the App Store, gaining increasingly impressive reviews with every new update Castelnuovo submitted. If there's one thing that characterizes

Pocket God, it's the game's constant references to pop culture and Internet memes. Everything from the Double-Rainbow YouTube video sensation to Charlie Sheen's public breakdown has been worked into the *Pocket God* universe. There have also been clever cross-promotional collaborations with other apps, like *Moron Test* and *Harbor Master*. Castelnuovo is a master at taking the fabric of popular social memes and weaving them into the *Pocket God* universe. Millions of players wait eagerly for every new update to discover what zeitgeisty new treat the game designers have worked into the latest installment.

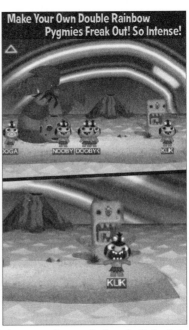

Pocket God is constantly updated with references to the latest pop-culture trends. Here, the *Pocket God* universe is paid a visit by the Double Rainbow from the viral YouTube video of the same name.

"We put a *Donkey Kong*-style of game in there," says Castelnuovo. "We also did *Ape Mountain* with a sacrificial altar where you can string an Oog up and he gets eaten. We've really tried to interact with other developers, other cultural items. We just did a Charlie Sheen update, and the Charlie Sheen Oog likes to have a monkey on his back, and he doesn't eat food, and no one trusts him when they sleep."

"We do whatever is entertaining to us. It's about energy and a sense of humor. The whole purpose is to drop in memes and kill in different ways. If we think it's funny, we put it into the game. The converse of that is that we put in full-on mini-games that aren't cultural, but are something unique we came up with. We might stick a role-playing game system in the game. Whatever we feel like! It's our creative outlet. Let's see how random and crazy we can get."

It's the kind of playful approach that you suspect would have been stifled in a traditional games studio. Because Castelnuovo developed *Pocket God* in such a small team, he was free of the criticism and interference of a traditional games studio. It's a freedom that he is acutely aware of.

THE GOD OF SMALL THINGS

"I had a stage where I tried to get an office and 10 people working for me," says Castelnuovo. "That wasn't that satisfying because of the management headaches and having to hire people. I'm much more comfortable working on my own, doing my own thing. I don't enjoy working on large scale projects."

"When the [software development kit] for the iPhone came out, I realized, 'Here is an opportunity to do exactly what I want. I can do the really small-team projects that I love to do, make money at it.' Plus, I had actual hardware. This [iPhone] can function like a console. I knew I had to get into it somehow. It seemed like the perfect time for it. [It was like] the docom bubble, I thought: 'I should do this.' But then you're like, 'Damn! Someone else did it.' This was one of those things where I thought if I made a point to get involved [before it was too late], I could end up being successful at it. I'm a pretty realistic guy... I think that success in the entertainment industry has a lot to do with luck: the reception of the audience. You can't really quantify or second guess that easily, so I knew that there was always going to be a chance. It's like a lottery ticket. The strategy was to keep it small, stay in the game for a long time, and keep working on projects until something stuck."

PERSISTENCE AND SELF-BELIEF

Castelnuovo certainly has persistence. He started his first iPhone app development project as "a little self-test to see what I could do in 10 hours." Eventually, *Pocket God* would develop as result of Castelnuovo's personal realization that he was unable to concentrate on any one project for very long. Far from disheartening him, he used this character trait to his advantage.

"I always had this problem," says Castelnuovo. "I try to do more than I can handle. I used to think: 'Oh my god I want to make *World of Warcraft* on the iPhone! I want to make a role-playing game with 60 hours of gameplay!' Then a month into the project I'd think: 'I want to make a retro shooter with special effects!'"

Castelnuovo didn't want to be in a situation where he was distracted from a project half way through; he wanted to keep it manageable. He decided that whatever he could do in 10 hours he would release on the App Store. He would learn the iPhone programming language, get the code written, and submit his app. In the process he could figure out what it took to submit software to Apple.

His first project was a simple special-effects program for the iPhone. Castelnuovo put in a couple of hours "porting the math over" and worked the app into a decent shape. It ended up selling 150 copies a day. "I could see if I get 10 of these things together I could probably pay for all my expenses," remembers Castelnuovo.

He spent a few more days improving the app, only to discover it was now selling just one or two copies a day.

THE EVOLUTION OF *POCKET GOD*

"Let's come up with a super idea," Castelnuovo decided. "For this project I wanted to do a week-long sprint between Christmas and New Years and see what we could do. At the time *Koi Pond* was doing pretty well and I thought: 'Wouldn't it be cool to do a sandbox app like *Koi Pond*, where you can't really do much at first, but we can add to it over time.' We came up with *Pocket God.*"

The evolution of *Pocket God* from its initial release to global blockbuster is particularly interesting because it demonstrates, more than any other app, how successful a developer can become if they listen closely to users and carefully adds incremental updates. *Pocket God* was a gradual success that won the hearts of millions of iPhone owners.

"At first *Pocket God* wasn't nearly as mean at it is now. You could take the Oogs and throw them in the air. I didn't really think about the death aspect of it. But then I thought it would be fun if you could stuff them in the water and watch them drown. People responded to it. The first sales data we got showed 300 to 500 copies sold a day and we thought, 'Wow, there's something here!'"

"We ran up against a lot of resistance early on. People were complaining there was not enough to do — not enough content. They said *Pocket God* was boring after 30 seconds. It forced us to really talk to the community and address their concerns and see if we could build a little wave."

"Touch Arcade was the first place we started talking to the community and put out an email to users, letting them know, 'We see what your concerns are.' Some users were challenging whether we were a sham company designed to rip people off. I had two other apps that weren't doing well at all. I explained that with *Pocket God* it was a different thing. We were going to put time and effort into it and we wanted to get their ideas. I said, 'We're going to do an update every week, at least for the first two or three weeks, and we'll see how it goes from there.' "

WEEKLY UPDATES DROVE UP SALES

The weekly updates worked wonders for *Pocket God* and lured users in droves. Castelnuovo thinks the public responded to the rapid serialization of the app because "it was like watching a TV show." *Pocket God* played on the same impulse people feel to watch the latest episode of their favorite television program each week.

"After a week, it was not too long that people forgot about *Pocket God*. It was the perfect timeframe to put out another update. Users were always looking forward to what was coming the next weekend. We ended up doing that for 14 weeks straight. We never got much publicity on review sites, or any promotion from Apple. It was all grassroots support. And then, after about two months, *Pocket God* broke into the top 10. We stayed for an entire month at the number one spot!"

CRAZY AND WACKY

Pocket God has slipped down the charts since then, but app sales have remained strong. *Pocket God* still dances around the top 50 U.S. iPhone games and the top 100 in Europe. Castelnuovo is about to release a universal version of the app — one that works on both the iPhone and the iPad app. Like other Appillionaires, he relishes the freedom success has brought.

"It's cool having our own property that we are free to do what we want with. More traditional companies are too cautious with their apps. They feel they can't ruin it and they have to stay true to what the original game is."

It's a playful attitude that gives *Pocket God* its unpredictable appeal. Castelnuovo says he doesn't want to be in a position where a corporate hierarchy dictates his creative decisions. And with *Pocket God* selling in the millions, he doesn't have to.

"If we come up with some insane idea and a user looks at it and says: 'How… Why are you guys doing that?' Well, it entertains us," says Castelnuovo. "We want to make people scratch their heads and say, 'Wow, that *Pocket God* is kind of crazy and wacky; I don't know how they stay in business.'"

THE LIFE AND TIMES OF CASTELNUOVO

Castelnuovo's story is interesting because his background in console hardware and the Sega Genesis would appear to be the opposite of the sales model the iPhone uses. Console games were sold on cartridges in shops by large publishers. But, in fact Castelnuovo finds the two experiences eerily similar.

"Consoles were harder. And, sure, back then it was more of a mess," says Castelnuovo. "You had to have a publisher if you were doing something for Sega or Nintendo, but the teams were small. *Clay Fighter* — for example — was a long project, but just two people worked on it. So I think there are a lot of similarities between development for the old consoles and what I do now."

But over time, Castelnuovo watched as game projects got bigger and bigger, and the industry ended up with projects like *Grand Theft Auto*, which "had a thousand people" working on it and, Castelnuovo says, turned him off the game industry.

"I liked the Sega Genesis and the Atari Jaguar," says Castelnuovo. "I liked messing around with the 3D hardware on the Sega Saturn. But at that point the teams started getting bigger, and the jobs got more specialized. I got out of there at that point. I don't really like that kind of thing. I like to be able to wear many hats. I liked the days of the Sega Genesis where you could have one programmer who does a lot of really cool things and these short projects that you can blaze through."

Castelnuovo stepped out of the console scene and began work on Flash projects where he had more control of the code. When the iPhone came along, it sparked the same passion he felt for the Genesis.

"You could suddenly do a lot of really cool stuff with the iPhone… I think it's more like the old days of the console. You have guys like Jeff Minter [a cult-favorite British programmer]. Today's generation of iPhone hardware is perfect for him. It's what he's been looking for his entire life: complete control of his game and distribution. Suddenly he can do that."

THE TERROR OF SUCCESS

I ask Castelnuovo how success has changed him. Very little, he thinks.

"I try to be a little bit Zen about it: Although we're up there in the charts, we could stay another day, or we could drop off… It's a lot of stress: when you're in the top five or number one you're checking the app store every five seconds, you're in a panic the whole time: 'How long can we stay there? When will we lose our momentum?' It took a good six months for us to get comfortable with the fact that we had something that had some longevity".

THE IMPORTANCE OF HARD WORK

As for many Appillionaires, for Castelnuovo the thrill of being number one was overshadowed by the amount of work involved in sustaining that level of success.

"Definitely there was a huge sense of excitement, but we were overworked too," he remembers. "The first 14 updates that we did, both me and Allen Dye [the artist on *Pocket God*] still had contracting jobs. I was putting in 80 hours a week at my day job, and we were cranking out a *Pocket God* update every week. It was new code, it wasn't just a new level. We were doing brand-new art, adding brand new functionality."

The team put out new game mechanics every single update. They would work during the week for clients. Around the middle of the week they would come up with a new idea for *Pocket God*. Then, usually on Thursdays, Castelnuovo would do investigation into the physics and reality of new game elements.

"If we were going to make a hurricane — for example — I'd need an algorithm to show the wind in the air, the wind lines," says Castelnuovo. "So, I'd get hold of a couple of articles that pointed me in that direction. By Friday we'd finish that off. On Saturday I'd do the bulk of the work, on Sunday we'd polish it and beta test it and submit it by 4am. On Monday, we would try and recover, get as much of our client work done as we could. Then the next Wednesday we would start the process all over again. There was a sense of exhilaration. It was really awesome — but we were so overworked that it was hard to take time off and have a celebration dinner."

Pocket God became so successful that Castelnuovo progressively took an extra day off his previous job. First reducing it to a four-day week, then three, then two, then one. Then he left.

"Once we were number one it was pretty obvious that we had enough money saved that we wouldn't be able to do better than this in our contract jobs even with a year of work. We were number one for a month and it was easy to say, 'Yeah, we can do this full time.'"

THE PUBLIC'S REACTION

Castelnuovo's success has propelled him into pop culture. Castelnuovo gave his mother a *Pocket God* statue, and when her assistant's son came round and spotted the statue he "was freaking out, he had no idea I made the game. He took his picture with it."

"When we go to Comic-Con [the world's biggest big comic convention], we get a pretty good response. A lot of people come along and we get to see a lot of kids and fans of *Pocket God* — that's pretty cool. I would say we definitely had our five minutes of fame, which is kind of neat."

STOP PITCHING ME!

Castelnuovo has also witnessed his fair share of elevator pitches from wannabe app developers. Both his accountant and his landscaper are constantly pitching him app ideas.

"It's funny because, being an app developer, everybody has an idea all of a sudden," says Castelnuovo. "That's common now, at all levels of app development. People see that a lot of people are making money, and that a lot of people have these devices. They think they could come up with an idea. But having an idea is 5 percent of the thing, implementation counts for a lot."

"It one of the most common things I run into now: The accountant sees the money we're making from this game and thinks: 'I need to get into that. It would be great if you partnered with me.'"

I tell Castelnuovo I experienced the same thing after the success of *Alice* and compare it to when a doctor arrives at a dinner party and all the guests start asking his advice on various ailments. They can't resist that engagement. So, if you say you're an app designer, they can't resist pitching you an app idea. I explain there's a disparity between the public perception of an app developer and how much work and luck it takes to have a success. The public tends to see the media fantasy of the gold rush and want to dive in. But Castelnuovo thinks I'm too pessimistic.

"It's not easy," he says. "But a lot of experienced developers are saying: 'Oh the gold rush is over, unless you get a big article on *Gizmodo*, unless you get a promo from Apple, it's over, there's no way to make money on it'. But that's simply not true."

"I think that you have to realize that success in an entertainment industry takes a lot of luck. Sure if you have a name, if you're Stephen Spielberg — for example— I'll go and see your movie because you're Stephen Spielberg. But he couldn't rely on that for his first movie."

"The best strategy is keep your costs down, and support your app like crazy. Be laser-focused in getting it out there. You can't just do something, watch it and see if it takes. You have to put everything behind it. Get a sense if the audience is receptive to your idea. If they're not, then cut your losses and work on a new game. But if there is enthusiasm, get behind it."

LUCK IS PART OF THE FORMULA

And luck?

"Okay, it takes a lot of luck," Castelnuovo says. "But I think implementation is important. You can have a good or a bad idea, but if the implementation is right, you can make a go of it. I think the easiest way to come up with a creative idea is to take an idea that everyone thinks is bad and make it cool: give it a really kick ass implementation and it may take off. *Enviro Bear* is a good example; there's a game where all the production values are crap, the reason why it works is that it's beautiful in its crappiness. You can have the best idea in the world, but if you don't pull it off right, nobody is going to care."

If there's one thing for me that characterizes *Pocket God* it's that it is heartfelt. There's no sterile corporate vision behind it. It looks like Castelnuovo has just done what he thought would be funny. I ask if he can rationalize what made the game such a success, or if he just acted on instinct.

"It's a hard question to answer. A lot of it was reception of the audience. *Pocket God* is heartfelt, it's genuine, it is legitimately what we think is cool and that resonates with a lot of people. A big part of any success is the receptivity of the audience."

"Have you heard of this book called *He's Just Not Into You?*" Castelnuovo asks me. "Well, the girl is wondering why the guy isn't into her. Is it my looks or my personality, she wonders. The book basically suggests it's neither of those things in particular and maybe he's just not that into you. I think that's the way the audience relates to apps. You can have the best team around, you can have all the things you need for success. You can have the right business people. But if the audience just isn't into your app they're not going to buy it. Maybe you have a spike when you have your big marketing push, when you get attention from the review websites. But it's not going to stick."

"On the converse you can get a really crappy app, like some of the line drawing apps, stick-figure type apps, and people just eat them up. They happen to be receptive to that kind of art style. The main thing is that we happened to be lucky. Beyond that we just work hard. We put out something honest, genuine and funny, it's all geared towards me and Allan Dye being the audience. We think: what can we do to make us laugh?"

Perhaps this is one of the most powerful assets of any creative person. It's incredibly useful if the audience in your head tallies with the desires of the audience out there. Beyond the hard work and ingenious design, perhaps some deep neurological instinct means, as humans, we love to drown Oogs in the water off the coast of a virtual desert island. It's a wholly unpredictable impulse to capitalize on, but Castelnuovo has done just that. Who would have guessed?

SUMMARY

Here's a roundup of the important points covered in this chapter:

- *Pocket God* was, like many successful apps, the end result of many years experience in programming and design. Castelnuovo worked his way up from college dropout, to lead programmer on a Sega game, and then to one of the world's best-loved iPhone games programmers. Castelnuovo took his experience inside the industry and used it to create his own work, taking advantage of the App Store's global reach. He's an inspiration to programmers who feel trapped inside a corporation. If this sounds like you: get out of there!

- Castelnuovo's only guiding principle has been to create work that amuses him personally. *Pocket God* didn't attempt to second-guess the market, but instead the game is a heartfelt expression of the designer's personality. *Pocket God* is one of the best examples of a game that could never have been built within the traditional studio system. Castelnuovo would not have been able to justify his design decisions to a committee — most of his game goes way beyond any rational thought process. The magic of *Pocket God* is that it somehow works, despite being born of Castelnuovo's brilliantly chaotic whims.

- The world of *Pocket God* feels alive and unlike many traditional games. Castelnuovo goes out of his way to include popular culture and Internet memes in the Pacific Island world that his creatures inhabit. As a result, gamers feel a particular excitement and attachment to the peculiar world the game presents. It's never clear quite what will happen next and the unusual mix of clever gameplay with topical comedy is a format that did not really exist before the App Store automated software updates in such a streamlined fashion. In effect, Castelnuovo has reinvented the serialized novels of Dickens — providing his readers, in this case gamers, an ever-changing and expanding narrative to enjoy in staggered installments.

- Castelnuovo is honest enough to concede that luck plays a large part in the success of any iPhone app. It's impossible to predict the mood of a global audience and the App Store is a tough market. There may be slim hope of building a hit app but, unless you at least try, there is no hope at all. Follow Castelnuovo's example and you'll have more of a chance than most.

9

STICKWARS

SOMEWHERE IN THE world, 1,000 feet or so beneath the surface of the ocean, you'll find John Hartzog, creator of the hit iPhone app *StickWars*. Today, Hartzog is an officer in the U.S. Navy where he is part of a submarine crew. His job involves navigation and managing the sub's on-board nuclear reactor. Of all the Appillionaires, Hartzog is the only one to have graduated from tinkering with the iPhone handset to controlling atomic hardware. If you thought your eight-core MacPro was a cool development platform, take a look at Hartzog's nuclear marine propulsion system and weep. His new occupation does make it harder for him to update the *StickWars* app, though.

"Now I spend a lot of time in a metal tube under the water. The WiFi is horrendous down there; it never ever works," Hartzog jokes. "Something to do with the several feet of steel between you and everything around you. It kills all reception."

John Hartzog, submarine officer and creator of *StickWars*, pictured here with his wife.

SOURCE: Reproduced with permission of John Hartzog © 2011 John E. Hartzog.

DEFENDING THE CASTLE

Hartzog created the smash-hit app *StickWars* during the brief time between the final days of college and his enrollment in the Navy. It's a castle-defense game where the aim is to protect your castle as waves of attackers attempt to storm the stronghold. You fling the attackers away with your fingers. When the game begins, you're left to defend the castle by the speed of your finger reflexes alone, but as the levels progress you can entrap archers and wizards to protect the walls. The process involves coaxing marauders into a prison from which you can then "recruit" members to defend the castle. If you're upset by gnarly scenes of violence you can tone down the amount of visible blood in the game's settings — you would, however, have to be unnaturally queasy if you felt any deep sympathy for the game's iconic stick-figure characters. They're basic human-like forms that give the game a warm, homemade charm.

StickWars is a castle defense game. Players must use their fingers to attack the aggressive invaders.

"I thought it would be really fun to have a game where you throw things around the screen," says Hartzog. "I was playing other games that were similar but the motion wasn't very smooth. These games were almost fun, but ultimately not satisfying in the way they were implemented. I thought I could put something better together in a few weeks, and I did."

Hartzog has always been "the crazy computer science guy."

THE EARLY YEARS

"I technically sold my first piece of software when I was 13 years old," he says. "Well, I say sold, but I had to give it away for free in the end. It was a Visual Basic app and it was a security system I designed to stop my brother and sister from using my computer. I put it up on a shareware website and started getting requests to buy it, but I was only 13 and couldn't set up a credit card transaction system."

Computers had always been a part of Hartzog's life. He loved science and programming, but says that he always had a feeling that computer programmers wouldn't be making much money by the time he left college, so he decided to join the Navy instead.

"As far as I could see, all the jobs were getting outsourced," Hartzog says. "So my focus was elsewhere. I love coding, I really do, but I'm dreading the day I get out of the Navy in three years and go looking for a job; I worry there won't be any great programming jobs out there."

Perhaps he doesn't have to worry if he can keep putting out apps like _StickWars_.

WAITING TO SURFACE

Hartzog began building _StickWars_ in 2009. The game was completed shortly after he graduated from college in May that year and he continued to update the app even when the Navy enlisted him full-time. Because, as Hartzog puts it, he "had no social life at the time" it was possible for the young submarine officer to keep updating his app in spare moments during training, although he has now turned that responsibility over to people who spend less time submerged in the depths of the ocean. iPhone gamers aren't generally used to waiting for their developer's submarine to surface before an app can be updated.

"*StickWars* was my first attempt at making a game for the iPhone," says Hartzog. "The App Store had been around for a while and there were games that I imagined would be fun to play on a touchscreen — especially one so responsive. But when I saw what games were out there, I realized: 'Wow! These are really, really bad.'"

Hartzog decided he would hide himself away and code like a bandit to create something better.

"My patient girlfriend, who is now my wife, let me sit in my dorm room all day long and code. I had to do a lot to make it work. I stayed in my room for quite literally days, doing the classes I needed to and programming the game."

TAKING A GAMBLE

Encouraged by the lack of competition in the early days of the App Store, Hartzog set about making the kind of game that he himself would have enjoyed playing. It took him just three weeks to get the first version of *StickWars* made and on the App Store. He hoped to capture iPhone gamers' appetite for direct-manipulation of the characters on-screen. Unlike many games at the time, *StickWars* let players physically grab and throw the stick figures around. Today the mechanic seems like a logical use of the iPhone technology, but back then it was rare to find a game that used stick-figure physics in a compelling and — more importantly — well-polished format.

"It was interesting to have things flying around the screen in a way other games weren't doing it," says Hartzog. "The biggest games at the time were *Pocket God* and *iShoot*, but they weren't as interactive or as dynamic back then. *StickWars* provided more of a direct translation from touch to action."

Hartzog says he had no expectations of success when he launched *StickWars*. The only reason he was able to program the app is because he took advantage of Apple's offer to let developers download Xcode (the software programmers use to develop for the iPhone) for free. But when Hartzog came to submit to the App Store he would have to pay the full developer's fee. Amazingly, at the time, he thought he was probably throwing his money away.

"I was super worried because it was $99 to sign up. I was seriously concerned that I would not get my $99 dollars back in app sales. I thought, 'What a potential waste here, blowing my money on this.' Up to that point it had all been a hobby. That was my state of mind at the time. I had been doing it for fun."

"StickWars was a fun game; my computer science buddies were entertained by it. But I had no idea how it would be received by the public. When it sold hundreds of copies, I realized it was something much bigger than I'd imagined."

DOUBLING THE CONTENT

StickWars raced up the App Store charts and it became clear that Hartzog had a hit on his hands. As the app climbed, Hartzog continued adding more and more content, rapidly increasing the value and popularity of the game. He estimates that the game content was doubled in those first few weeks.

"The tipping point was when it hit the top 100. Then I knew that *StickWars* was going to be a massive success," says Hartzog. "It was a sweet deal. I didn't celebrate yet, but I stopped going out with my friends and just worked solidly on it."

"I kept cranking away at it. I hit a momentum and realized that, if I kept updating the app every three weeks, I could accelerate the rise," he says. "I added a ton of stuff to the game, because after just being on the store for a couple of weeks, it was selling many hundreds of copies and I thought: 'this is really worth my time.' Of course, I was also doing it for fun."

Unlike some app developers, Hartzog makes a very clear diagnosis of why *StickWars* met such a warm reception from the iPhone owning masses. It was, in his view, a fortunate combination of being first to market with a seamless control system for throwing around the stick figures, but also aiming for a much higher quality of app than his competitors had managed to put out.

COCOS2D SAVES THE DAY

"There were no other apps at the time that responded to touch in a natural and fluid way. With StickWars you could drag your finger as quickly as you could and the game reacts quickly without jerking. The characters behave as you'd expect a figure to respond in a physics environment. It was far above the level of any touch games available at the time."

Hartzog makes an interesting observation, and one that seems to hold true for all the Appillionaires. Not only did the most successful app designers come up with interesting ideas, but the touch-input system for their apps seems to have been uniquely well crafted. Whether it's the super-smooth animation of *Doodle Jump*, the graceful line drawing in *Harbor Master*, or the satisfying trajectory traced by an *Angry Birds* character, there is a running theme: The best apps seem to pay attention to the tiniest details of the finger mechanics used to operate them. There was also one other essential ingredient that Hartzog relied on.

"The large reason why I was able to do this is because of the Cocos2d library," he says.

Cocos2d is a free library of pre-built graphics code that developers can use to save themselves hours of coding and experimentation. Instead of writing hundreds of lines of code to simulate gravity, for example, you can use a Cocos2d library to automate the process in a single line.

"When I look back it was fortunate timing. If I'd started in 2008 it wouldn't have worked; I would have had to code all the Cocos2d stuff myself," says Hartzog. "There's a lot of work needed to create realistic physics sims. Luckily, by March the library of Cocos2d code was there to use. I was able to grab it in a near-finished state — just one month earlier and I would have had to recreate all the work. Cocos2d was a big factor in the success of *StickWars*. It was very lucky that a free Open Source graphics library was being created in parallel with my app."

A LIFE AT SEA

At the height of *StickWars'* success, Hartzog was pulling 12-hour days, 7 days a week, working constantly on the app. His attention to *StickWars* gradually waned as his military career began to take over, but he was lucky enough to have had enough downtime to push updates during brief gaps in his training and used it to make tweaks to the *StickWars* universe.

Hartzog thinks the success of *StickWars* has changed his life very little. His decision to join the Navy was pre-*StickWars*, so in many ways his future was already mapped out.

"I knew what I wanted to do before I made *StickWars*," says Hartzog. "I love working with computers and I love building things, but I didn't want to be an iPhone dev all my life. I wouldn't quit the Navy to become another iPhone developer."

"Anyway, I can't really just say 'I quit the navy!'" he laughs. "I have a company now that has an amazing product and great relationships with other developers. We're continuing to launch stuff, and occasionally I can help, but in terms of day to day, my commitment is to the Navy."

What does Hartzog make of the rise of the bedroom programmer and the fact he was able to sell his app to a global audience?

"I think it's fantastic," he says. "When you think about it we've had the technology to allow us to do this for 10 years. The only reason I couldn't sell the software I wrote when I was 13 were the legal, technical and financial barriers. There just wasn't a convenient distribution system for software. Now you have people who can write fantastic software in their bedroom. One person working for a few weeks can make something amazing. Before Apple came along, things were tough for individual programmers."

Hartzog says he was hugely inspired and influenced by Sean O'Connor, a British games programmer. O'Conner was a rare bedroom-developer success story well before the App Store. He made software for Palm OS, the Palm Pilot, and the PC and became a cult-programming icon in the late 90s. O'Connor was once in similar situation to Hartzog.

"O'Connor had a job as programmer, but he started making games on side," says Hartzog. "He eventually made so much money he quit his job and became a successful bedroom programmer. It was fascinating to watch that happen years ago. He is a very inspiring figure for me — someone who just enjoys making games and does it so well can make a career out of it."

"It is so much harder now," says Hartzog of the current app scene. "I can't imagine what it's like for those coming in as new independent developers. It can still be done — you can still build a hit app — but the number of indie developers appearing in the top of charts is very quickly dwindling. It's getting more competitive."

"When I worked on *StickWars*, I did all the coding and design all myself, but after I reached that tipping point where the app was successful, I hired a friend to work on the graphics for me, and some people to create the soundtrack — things I couldn't flesh out myself."

"I was lucky because *StickWars* was an early success. I had demonstrated that I could make money before I had to invest money. I knew I would get a paycheck at the end of month, so I could pay to improve the graphics and sound. But people are taking a big risk now. They're putting that money up front. You could easily spend $10,000 or more to make a game that totals just $100 in sales."

As with the other Appillionaires, it seems like Hartzog simply enjoys applying himself wholeheartedly to the task at hand. Clearly he's driven by a love of technology, and I can't help but wonder if the App Store just wasn't exciting enough for him. Given a choice between programming casual iPhone games for middle-class commuters, or piloting a nuclear submarine across the seven seas, he's probably taken the more exciting option. It's unlikely that many *StickWars* gamers know that the man who created the app is submerged in the belly of a steel beast, patrolling the waters, but next time you see someone playing the app you might point it out.

SUMMARY

Here's a roundup of the important points covered in this chapter:

- Hartzog's advice to someone who wants to give it a shot? "Work independently. That's what I did at the start. Focus on making a fantastic game and worry about money later. First, make a great product."

- Hartzog doesn't get much time to work on apps these days, and his job in the Navy couldn't be further from a programming task. Today he deals with the physical engineering realties of a nuclear submarine reactor and his responsibilities navigating the deep ocean. If there's a lesson to be drawn from this it's follow your heart. Hartzog still dabbles in apps, but he knew when to walk away.

- I asked Hartzog if his experiences in the military might inspire a future iPhone game? "Maybe," he told me. "At the moment I'm just enjoying what I do." If you're an app designer, you should look for inspiration in the world around you. The more unusual and adventurous your everyday life, the more ideas you'll have for a great app. Don't obsess over app ideas, but keep an eye out.

- *StickWars* demonstrates that simple artwork can be extremely effective in a popular iPhone title. Don't make the mistake of assuming that iPhone gamers are married to a particular polished look. Just like *Doodle Jump*, *StickWars* embraces its homemade roots. App makers should be bold and honest with their app designs.

10 ANGRY BIRDS

THE ELASTIC OF the catapult groans under pressure. Suddenly it snaps furiously back, releasing a small bird high into the blue sky of the Pacific Ocean. Faster and higher the bird climbs, now just a speck above the island below. For a moment it seems suspended in space. Then slowly, delightfully, it reaches the peak of its trajectory and begins to fall to the ground, tracing an elegant arc through the air.

Smash! The bird collides with a wooden castle on the island's surface. The beams of the castle wobble and creak. For a moment it looks like the structure will hold, but then the bird tumbles down the outer wall, knocking out a vital support beam. The castle shudders and collapses, instantly killing its inhabitants: two green pigs.

The bird squawks for a moment — perhaps shocked by its involuntary slaughter of the pigs — it then sheds a few feathers and, without any particular fanfare, gently explodes.

This surrealist fantasy is a description of the game *Angry Birds*, one of the best-selling titles in the history of videogames. It's an astonishing achievement for a game that its creators, Rovio, initially regarded as a flop in the App Store's biggest markets.

A GLOBAL HIT

Recently, the *Guinness Book of World Records* has recognized *Angry Birds* as the top paid app store game; it has been downloaded over 250 million times and continues to average an unfathomable 1 million downloads every single day. Rovio claims to have data that demonstrates gamers across the world collectively spend a staggering 200 million minutes per day playing *Angry Birds* on their devices — and over 1 million hours per day on iOS devices alone.

"Think of all the other stuff they could be doing that's so much more boring," said Mikael Hed, CEO of Rovio, when confronted with this enormous expenditure of global man-hours. "Nowadays, people have to be entertained all the time, whenever you have just a few moments spare... much of those 200 million minutes comes from this type of micro spare time, filling the little gaps."

It's a perfectly rational argument, and world governments agree with him. *Angry Birds* is the only iPhone game to have been publicly endorsed by heads of state. *The Telegraph* reported that British Prime Minister, David Cameron, is "a huge *Angry Birds* fan" and "uses his iPad to play the game which involves catapulting wingless and legless birds to destroy green pigs trying to eat their eggs."

Russian president, Dmitry Medvedev, has publicly thanked Rovio's marketing leader Peter Vesterbacka for his work on the game. At the International Economic Forum in St. Petersburg, Medvedev stood up and made an announcement to the audience:

> *"Before talking politics, I would like to thank Mr. Vesterbacka for creating an occupation for a huge number of officials who now know what to do in their free, and not-so-free, time. I saw them playing [Angry Birds] myself many times."*

Beyond its influence on global politics, the game has made its impact felt throughout society. *Angry Birds* has a celebrity fan club that includes such improbable luminaries as author Salmon Rushdie (who proclaimed he was "something of a master at *Angry Birds*") satirist Jon Stewart, and comedian Conan O'Brien.

O'Brien went so far as to build a working replica of the game out of Ikea furniture and break it apart on his show.

"We have decided to honor, tonight, Finland's greatest contribution to mankind," Conan began his set piece. "I'm talking, of course, about the videogame, *Angry Birds*." He then proceeded to smash the life-size game to pieces by firing inflatable *Angry Birds* at the furniture.

Teen pop sensation Justin Bieber has also made his love of the game clear. For better or worse, Bieber is a social barometer for huge swathes of the North American teen population and Rovio could not have hoped for better publicity than when Bieber tweeted his open endorsement of the app: "I love the game *Angry Birds*. It's so sick."

More than any other iPhone game, *Angry Birds* has crept its way into the popular culture. There is something supernaturally compelling about the game mechanism — a psychological desire I'll return to later in this chapter — that keeps players coming back. This, coupled with cute character design and a strong game narrative, has made much of the iPhone owning population fall in love with these strange birds on their remote Pacific island. Rovio has capitalized on this affection for the characters and given physical reality to the birds in the app. You can buy merchandise from the line of *Angry Birds* stuffed toys — Rovio has already sold over 60,000 of them. Amazingly, it's estimated that nearly half of Rovio's revenue these days is from merchandise and licensing — goods that exist beyond the universe of the game itself.

52ND TIME LUCKY

Founded in 2004, and originally called Relude, Rovio is run by two Finnish cousins, Niklas and Mikael Hed. The company was initially funded by Mikael's father, the entrepreneur Kaj Hed, to the tune of 1 million — not that this money ultimately helped Rovio, they would burn through the cash well before glory hit. Although to the outside world it appears as if *Angry Birds* was an overnight success, the true story of Rovio is one of financial disaster, heartbreak, disappointment, 52-failed-games, and — most importantly — hard graft against the all the odds. Today *Angry Birds* sits perched on the roof of the App Store, the iconic iPhone success story, but before it got there the family-run Rovio would fall into commercial ruin, almost collapse, and narrowly dodge bankruptcy.

Mikael Hed, one of the two cousins behind the global blockbuster *Angry Birds*.
SOURCE: Reproduced with permission of Chillingo © 2011 Rovio Mobile.

TWO UNSTOPPABLE COUSINS

Mikael and Niklas, much like the *Doodle Jump* brothers, grew up with a fierce interest in creating videogames. The two cousins would discuss game ideas with each other throughout childhood. Niklas had a particular interest in physics games that he would code and show off to friends. His fascination with programming led to a Computer Science degree at Helsinki University, while his cousin Mikael served in the Finnish Army for a year before enrolling in business school — studying first in Europe, and then the United States.

After graduating, Niklas persuaded Mikael to join him in building a video games company to sell software to the mobile phone industry. These were the days before the iPhone, when every game contract had to be carefully and elaborately negotiated with individual cellphone carriers. It was a logistical nightmare and Mikael was initially reluctant to get involved.

But Niklas could be pretty persuasive. The young man was buoyed by his success in winning a competition to create a game for an early smartphone. He eventually convinced Mikael that, on the basis of this success, they could make a go of the mobile games market.

Niklas also had the blessing of Hewlett-Packard's influential communications wizard, Peter Vesterbacka.

THE VESTERBACKA FACTOR

Vesterbacka warmed to Niklas at the smartphone game competition Niklas had won in 2003. The event was sponsored by HP and Vesterbacka was a judge on the panel. He was extremely impressed by the work that Niklas had put in, telling him in no uncertain terms to "start your own mobile company." Little did he know it then, but seven years later, Vesterbacka would leave his job and join Rovio to control marketing plans at the height of the company's success.

Mikael rented space to work in and Relude began client work for other games developers. But conflicts with his father Kaj — the most substantial investor in the fledgling outfit — quickly turned the operation sour. By the middle of 2005, the situation became unworkable and Mikael quit the company, choosing to focus on publishing independent comic books instead.

Without Mikael to exert an influence on Rovio's direction, the company spiraled further into crisis. Although Rovio continued to win work from an impressive client roster including EA and Namco, there was a feeling inside the company that the hit game titles that were supposed to have been Rovio's focus would never materialize. As development costs piled up, Rovio strayed ever further from its initial plan. The company began to experience huge losses.

BURN MONEY, BURN

By the beginning of 2009, Rovio's finances were up in flames — portentous for a company whose Finnish name translates to "bonfire." In its darkest hour, Rovio was forced to slash its 50-person workforce to just 12. It was then that a sense of reality set in: Rovio had been conceived as a hit games company; the problem was, they had none. Just when it looked like the company had collapsed, Niklas had a revelation. He convinced Kaj to rehire Mikael, cede control of the company's direction to him, and move their focus away from client work. And the event that inspired this critical decision for the future of Rovio? It was the invention of the iPhone and the introduction of the Apple App Store.

Niklas recognized that the iPhone solved many of Rovio's problems. No longer would the company have to rely on the marketing teams of larger publishers, or deal with the bitter negotiation with cellphone carriers. The App Store meant worldwide distribution, and direct access to millions of customers. Apple would be their publishing arm, and they could concentrate on teasing out that deeply precious and frustratingly elusive gem: A hit app.

Client work for other games companies tided the company over temporarily. Then, in the Spring of 2009, Rovio's lead game designer, Jaakko Iisalo opened up Photoshop and began to draw a game screenshot. Iisalo would often pitch ideas to the team and this would be one of many ideas he had worked on for Rovio. He drew some colored birds and matched the color of each bird to a colored block. The idea was that tapping the colored block would cause a bird of the same color to bounce across and smash it. The screenshot looked like a shadow of the game *Angry Birds* would eventually become, but there was something to it, or so Iisalo thought.

The *Angry Birds* characters evolved from early sketches by Jaakko Iisalo.
SOURCE: Reproduced with permission of Rovio © 2011 Rovio Mobile.

Iisalo showed the screenshot to Niklas and Mikael who were instantly taken by the bird's angry faces and the absurdity of their flightlessness. The team decided to add pigs as the bird's enemy — coloring them green to imply swine-flu infection, and later creating a backstory accusing the pigs of stealing the bird's eggs — an explanation for the cruel attacks the player would have to subject them to.

In testing the game, the designers quickly discovered that every minor change to the code would result in the programmer getting helplessly absorbed in playing rounds of the game, rather than attending to the task at hand.

"With our earlier titles, most friends and family members had usually taken a cursory look at the games, and given some generally positive feedback," Mikael would explain later. "But with *Angry Birds* the response was nearly always the same — they took the iPhone, found a quiet nook, and played the game for an hour, before the phone could be pried out of their hands." This was seriously addictive stuff.

Many players found *Angry Birds* highly addictive from the start.

SOURCE: Reproduced with permission of Chillingo © 2011 Rovio Mobile.

A RICH HISTORY OF FLYING ANIMALS

The *Angry Birds* concept was ultimately not a wholly original invention — almost no great invention is — but Rovio's combination of gameplay elements in the game was both novel and outstanding. *Angry Birds* comes from a rich heritage of physics games that involve hurling objects through the air at collapsible structures — games like *Crush the Castle* and its precursor *Castle Cloud*. There are also numerous other animal-throwing games that contain elements of Angry Bird's physics mechanism, but fall far short of its sweet-spot combination of gameplay, characterization, and graphics — *Hedgehog Launch* and *Toss the Turtle*, for example, are earlier examples of creatures used as projectiles. However, although it's possible to point to these earlier games as significantly influential — and some of Rovio's detractors go further — these earlier games all contained single elements of what would become the whole of *Angry Birds*. It was only *Angry Birds* that combined these disparate game elements in such a universally satisfying format. The Rovio team's skill lay in recognizing what worked and adapting it, Mikael would later describe *Angry Birds* as "really the sum of all of its parts."

Examining the prototype of the game, back before launch, Rovio were thrilled with its addictive qualities: They thought they had a hit. Niklas and Mikael were convinced this would be the game to turn Rovio around; it would be a pay-off for years of chaos and uncertainty in the company. They decided to invest just over €100,000 into the development of the game and launched *Angry Birds* onto the App Store at the very end of 2009. That December, Rovio held its collective breath and watched to see what would happen.

Angry Birds flopped.

A TERRIBLE RECEPTION

The big markets — the U.S. and the UK — took a look, shrugged their shoulders at the game and ignored it. Shaken by the reaction, Rovio noticed something interesting: the smaller App Stores were easier to compete in. They decided to concentrate on these smaller stores before trying again with the biggest markets. Getting to the top of the App Store in Finland, for example, required only a few hundred sales per day, compared to the many thousand a game would need to achieve in the U.S. As Rovio concentrated its attention on them, other European countries followed suit — the company sold over 30,000 copies of *Angry Birds* in these smaller markets. Evidence of success in these territories would, Rovio thought, help convince Apple to promote their app. But rather than attempt to approach Apple on their own, Rovio decided to team up with the then-independent games publisher Chillingo.

Chillingo was a UK games developer that already had a reputation for high-quality apps and a relationship with Apple that would be invaluable in securing the last essential ingredient in the success of *Angry Birds*: a coveted promotional banner in the App Store.

TOTAL AVIAN DOMINATION

The persistence of Rovio and Chillingo caught Apple's attention and it was agreed between them that *Angry Birds* would be given a prized spot in the UK App Store as Apple's Game of the Week in the second week of February 2010. Niklas and Mikael saw this as a one-shot chance to push *Angry Birds* to the top of the charts. So, the cousins began a series of enhancements to the game, adding more than 40 new levels, building a lite (free) version of the game, and designing a YouTube trailer to promote it. Their campaign was strategically designed to impress the iPhone masses when Apple's promotion hit. And hit it did.

More and more levels were added, along with a lite version of the game.

SOURCE: Reproduced with permission of Chillingo © 2011 Rovio Mobile.

In the first week of the promotion, *Angry Birds* shot up the charts, from obscurity in the very lowest reaches of the games charts, and all the way to number one. The Hed cousins were stunned. But it was just the beginning; by April the same year the game was also at number one in the U.S. The *Angry Birds* phenomena had begun and there was no stopping it. The colorful birds that began life as a screenshot in Rovio's dour office block in Finland were now hurling their flightless bodies across the screen of every iPhone from Tokyo to Cairo — this was total avian domination. Simplicity and smart design had won over millions of fans.

"There's this old wisdom," Mikael told *GamePro*. "[A good game] has to be easy to pick up and play but hard to master. The 'easy to learn' part was really important to us. When you see one screenshot of the game you know what you have to do."

> *"Angry Birds is simple, but it still has depth. It has to be so much fun that players want to return to the game over and over again. Angry Birds achieved precisely that."*

BIGGER THAN THE IPHONE

Today it's estimated that Rovio has a yearly revenue in excess of around $80 million and stands alone as an App Store success story that has transcended the iPhone platform. The *Angry Birds* have fluttered their way into popular culture and even Hollywood. In what seems like the ultimate endorsement of Rovio's extraordinary success, the company was asked to make a tie-in game for 20th Century Fox's animated feature film, *Rio*. In this special edition of the app, *Angry Birds Rio*, the *Angry Birds* characters share a game universe with the film's animated heroes — it sold over 10 million copies in 10 days. This licensing deal is typical of Rovio's very cautious and intelligent approach to capitalizing on their hit game.

"We saw that most gaming companies had then immediately tried to make another hit game," Mikael explained to CNBC. "We realized that had very rarely worked. Rather, we started to look at what we could do around *Angry Birds* and if there was a way that we could build this into an entertainment franchise. Games are what we are very strong at, and we will do other games besides *Angry Birds* as well, but now as we are executing our media company strategy, we're not in a tremendous hurry to churn out game after game after game."

This focused approach has meant that *Angry Birds Rio* is just one of many themed editions that Rovio has created for the game, extending their flagship brand further and further into the popular consciousness. Others include a Halloween edition — in which the pigs are joined by pumpkins — and a summer edition called *Pignic*.

The Halloween edition.
SOURCE: Reproduced with permission of Chillingo © 2011 Rovio Mobile.

Now there is talk of an *Angry Birds* theme park.

"Believe it or not, we have had such suggestions, and I believe *Angry Birds* Land was actually the name they used," Mikael told Reuters. "Whether there will be a theme park dedicated to *Angry Birds* or not, I don't know, but I would be surprised if within 10 years there wouldn't be at least a theme park with something related to *Angry Birds* in it."

There's even an animated TV series in the works.

The merchandizing craze has enveloped *Angry Birds*, with T-shirts, stuffed animals, and more.

SOURCE: Reproduced with permission of Chillingo © 2011 Rovio Mobile.

"We have been looking at that for quite a while, and that is definitely one of my personal big focus areas right now — to work on broadcast content for *Angry Birds*," Mikael told *C21 Media Magazine* at the beginning of 2011.

Rovio struggled to sell the game to Android users — a notoriously difficult market to retail software in — so gave it away for free. They now rack up around $1 million each month from pure advertising revenue on the platform.

SETTING THE APP STANDARD

More than any other game, *Angry Birds* is responsible for the public perception that app designer is one of the hottest jobs on the planet right now. Videogames were always creeping towards the status of Hollywood blockbusters, but with budgets to match. *Angry Birds* — despite the harsh and difficult reality of its birth — looks simple to the outside observer. In part it's the deceptive accessibility of this game design that has inspired so many others to give the App Store a shot. It's also elevated the games programmer to a status of social acceptability that has historically escaped them. We have the exploding birds to thank.

Angry Birds seems like a romantic story of easy success, but it's not.

SOURCE: Reproduced with permission of Chillingo © 2011 Rovio Mobile.

SUMMARY

Here's a roundup of the important points covered in this chapter:

- *Angry Birds* was not an overnight success. The Hed cousins took 52 tries until they created their hit app and in the process the company was almost destroyed.

- *Angry Birds* took an existing game paradigm — the castle and catapult format — and polished and evolved it. In retrospect it's easy to point to the reasons why *Angry Birds* is so compelling, but the simplicity of the game's execution is deceptive. It's *hard* to make something look *this easy*. Rovio is a great example of a small app company who took the time to build a quality product and teamed up with the right people to market it. The results were spectacular.

- Rovio saw the value of good marketing. The company didn't attempt to take on the app market alone; they sought the services of a much more experienced team to give their game the boost it needed. Creating a great app is just a small part of the equation. It's critically important to get your software seen by as many people as possible. If your app is addictive and well designed, you'll easily reap the rewards of more public exposure. However, you need to be sure that it's worth the time and money to promote. No amount of publicity will sell a bad app. Unlike Hollywood, where awful films can be pushed to profitability by a concerted marketing drive, app consumers are extremely fickle and demanding. There are literally thousands of other apps they could spend their money on if yours is not up to scratch.

- *Angry Birds* is the prime example of an app that successfully expanded its game universe beyond the iPhone hardware. Rovio organized tie-in deals with movie studios, and clothes and toy manufacturers. The *Angry Bird* characters exist in many different forms of merchandise and the company makes a considerable chunk of its profits outside the App Store, selling physical goods.

■ Rovio ran an interesting test case for the Android platform — the rival to Apple's iPhone. The company appears to have concluded that Android users are unlikely to pay for app software — *Angry Birds* is free on Android — but that decent profits can be made through in-app advertising banners. Whether this model is sustainable for non-superstar developers is a question that will be answered over the coming years.

THE APP REVOLUTION

11

FROM BEDROOM TO BOARDROOM

IN THE LAST few years, the iPhone and iPad have transformed many an indie programmer into a captain of industry. The ascent of the lone programmer from the bedroom to the boardroom is another side effect of the mass popularity of Apple's products.

In response to the success of software sales on the iPhone, larger investment conglomerates and multi-national games companies have been bodysnatching small indie studios in a frenzy of acquisitions. While some developers, like Mills at ustwo, resent the fact that the developer community is losing its spiritual heart to lumbering corporate giants, the indie acquisition is often a lucrative one. Many studios long for the day when the long tentacle of the vampire squid taps on the door and blows banknotes at them.

A GOLDEN AGE

There is a feeling across the industry that we may be living in that most unique of times: the blink of an eye at the beginning of many technological revolutions where the lucky few make decisions that will eventually lead to colossal fortunes.

Apple itself was begun in 1976 in a garage in Los Altos, California. The space had been used to restore cars by Jobs's father, but he cleared the it out for his son and Steve Wozniak to set up Apple Computers. Amusingly, a giant wood workbench — lugged home by Job's father — was Apple's first production line. "It was just the two of us, Woz and me," Jobs told *Fortune* magazine when he returned to the space years later. "We were the manufacturing department, the shipping department, everything."

Many iPhone programmers begin in similar circumstances — with little more than an iPhone, a MacBook from eBay, and some programming manuals. These simple electronic gadgets and some imagination are the only tools of those who have risen to superstardom as Appillionaires.

Then you add luck.

AN ESCAPE FROM CORPORATE TYRANNY

One such app superstar who made the transition from indie to world-domination and then got snapped up by a corporate giant is Simon Oliver, creator of the smash hit *Rolando*. After graduating, he spent several years building Flash projects for interactive agencies in London, but Oliver found himself tiring of working for clients and overtaken by a desire to create games. He decided that he wanted to work in the games industry. Oliver had played games since he was a youngster, but he quickly discovered that it was almost impossible, as a newcomer, to get a foot in the door of the existing games companies.

"It was pretty tough, as I was competing for jobs with candidates with much more industry experience and several console games under their belt," explained Oliver, "so I began to look for other routes to get into the industry and cut my teeth. The indie games scene was really exploding, with titles like *World of Goo* and *Braid* demonstrating that small teams with a great idea can create hugely successful games."

Simon Oliver, creator of *Rolando*, escaped the nine-to-five drudgery of his programming job and found fame and fortune as an independent iPhone developer.

SOURCE: Reproduced with permission of Simon Oliver © 2011 Simon Oliver.

These two titles, among others, were something of a revelation for the games industry. It came as a shock to some traditional games companies that consumers were after a simple, enjoyable and non-complex gaming experience.

Such gamers didn't necessarily care for 3D graphics, or elaborately plotted storylines. They just wanted to have fun. The mutually supportive relationship between games companies and hardware manufacturers had, for years, encouraged a reckless escalation of the complexity of games, driving hardware upgrade cycles. The buzzwords of the age were "immersive" and "realistic," and to a great extent the casual gamer was ostracized. This was all to change.

Braid demonstrated how a very small team with a strong idea could create a devastatingly cool and addictive game. *Braid* quickly became highest-rated title on Xbox Live.

SOURCE: Reproduced with permission of Jonathan Blow © 2011 Number None, Inc.

ZERO BUDGET IS A HERO'S BUDGET

Against the backdrop of million-dollar budget games, Nintendo launched the Wii and, later, Apple launched the iPhone. Although these two platforms appear wildly different, they both had one very important thing in common: they celebrated gameplay over graphics, ushering in the now-fashionable movement towards stripped-down low-fi "fun-is-everything" romps. The effect on the industry was profound: it suddenly became viable for a small team to produce commercially successful games again. First, the Wii demonstrated that simple, well-executed titles could be popular. Next, the iPhone proved that these could be built cheaply and distributed on a massive scale. The skyrocketing budgets of the multinational games corporations began to look faintly comical. The bedroom was, after a decade-long hiatus, a place for programmers to make their fortunes again.

"When the iPhone was announced, something clicked, and I realized that this was the platform that I'd been waiting for - I was really excited," explained Oliver. "The very first App I worked on was an unreleased prototype called Duck Amuck. This was in November 2007, before the App Store was announced and before the SDK (Software Development Kit) was released. I was desperate to create something so I got playing with the unofficial SDK that some intrepid hackers had pulled together. It was a pretty basic game but great fun to get something up and running at such an early stage."

Oliver's experience is typical of many successful developers who got in at the start. He could not wait for Apple to open up development on the iPhone platform and so, after the official App Store and iPhone SDK was announced, but before the launch of the store, he started prototyping apps on hacked firmware (see Chapter 5).

"I went through a ton of different prototypes and variations," explained Oliver, "at this stage there was nothing to really compare to or use as reference. There was no App Store, no announced games, no established conventions for using the multitouch screen and accelerometer. I felt like I hit a dead end several times, but eventually worked through the major design problems." Eventually Oliver felt like he had a core idea that was strong enough to turn into a full game: *Rolando*.

THE WORLD OF *ROLANDO*

Rolando is a platform game where you play a round-shaped character who is able to spin along surfaces, propelled by a virtual gravity caused by the players rotating their iPhones or iPads. It's the type of gravity platformer that wouldn't have been possible to create until very recently. The accelerometer component — the bit of the iPhone that detects its orientation and motion in space — wasn't included in a mainstream gadget until the iPhone. The Sony PSP had a similar game title, *Loco Roko*, but Oliver was the first to popularize this game genre on the iPhone.

Oliver continued freelancing to support the early development of the title, but eventually decided to concentrate purely on creating the game, investing all his time and savings into its development. He started looking for an illustrator to create the visual side of the game, scouring illustration portfolios, blogs, and T-shirt sites, and eventually coming across the portfolio of Mikko Walamies, a young illustrator from Finland.

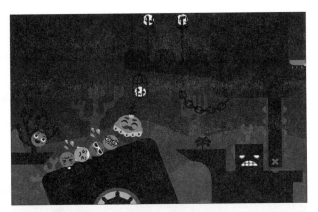

Rolando, Simon Oliver's furiously successful iPhone game, allows players to take control of a chubby circular fellow. The character is controlled by physically tilting your Apple device.

SOURCE: Reproduced with permission of Simon Oliver © 2011 ngmoco.

"I just loved the style of his work — so charming without the need for a great deal of detail," says Oliver, "Given the modest power of the first generation iPhone, we needed to employ a bold style that could communicate charm and character without needing a lot of horsepower."

Oliver put out a trailer for his game at the very beginning of July 2008. Within hours it was picked up by a huge number of news sites that, at the time, were desperate for any news about the kind of apps that would be coming to the iPhone.

NGMOCO ENTERS THE FRAY

A few days later the phone rang. It was Alan Yu from ngmoco, a then unknown U.S.-based and venture-backed publisher that had just started up, dedicated to creating and publishing games for the new platforms spearheaded by the iPhone. He wanted Oliver to fly out and meet the company in San Francisco.

"There was a really good chemistry there," says Oliver "we both saw the iPhone as an amazing opportunity that was going to make a big impact on the games industry."

ngmoco was formed by an ex-Electronic Arts executive Neil Young, using venture capital provided by the famous $200 million iFund announced at the launch of the App Store. ngmoco's plan was ingenious in its simplicity: the company would use venture capital to snap up promising indie developers and focus them on building profitable apps. ngmoco would eventually find investment of $40.6 million and achieve more than 7 million installs of their titles before the company itself was gobbled up in a $400 million acquisition by Japanese mobile games company DeNA.

Oliver started working with ngmoco a few weeks after his San Francisco meeting, and the team launched *Rolando* in December 2008.

"I remember getting up at 3am, when the game was due to go live and watching the first reactions come through," says Oliver, "there's only a few times that I can remember being more nervous. We'd delayed the launch a little, and there were some huge threads on forums of players discussing *Rolando* and awaiting it. I felt like it would be near impossible to meet their expectations."

When ngmoco executive Alan Yu was asked why the company didn't attempt their iPhone games business while still within EA, he told reporters, "EA is a great company, I love it and the people and I learned so much while I was there. But you can move faster when you are independent and not a part of those larger organizations… instead of 80-person teams working on a game that they hope will be a hit, you have two- to three-man teams — or in the case of *Rolando*, one guy — working on a release schedule that covers just a few months."

GodFinger by ngmoco, one of the company's considerable libraries of iPhone game titles.

Bizarrely, two years later, EA would freak out and begin an iPhone developer bodysnatch, swallowing down indie developers like Chillingo (*Angry Birds*) and Firemint (*Flight Control*). Apparently they are blind to the irony that their in-house policies were death to this kind of off-the-wall development.

While multi-national games companies like EA tend to stifle creativity with boardroom drudgery, indies like Oliver were highly motivated and, above all, excited.

"When Rolando finally went live, I was hooked on the forums and Twitter search, and so relieved to see such a positive reaction." says Oliver. "The first review we got was a 10 out of 10 from PocketGamer that morning and, from then on, I was able to relax a little. I spent most of the day in the pub celebrating, and glued to the App Store charts, as it eventually climbed into the top five."

INVASION OF THE BODY SNATCHERS

Alan Yu was asked back in July 2009 whether he thought the encroachment of companies like EA and Gameloft into the iPhone scene would upset ngmoco's plans.

"I think there's lots of room for all kinds of companies in this space," said Yu. "But the other advantage we have is understanding the user space and knowing how people use their iPhones. It's a benefit to us to solely focus on this device and not be distracted by other things the way bigger games publishers might."

A year after this interview, Yu and his board of executives sold ngmoco to DeNA, a corporation so vast and monolithic that shortly after the sale it was raided by the Fair Trade Commission under suspicion of violating Japan's Anti-Monopoly Act. So much for working outside the system. ngmoco, whether by design or accident, had bought up indies and then sold them straight back into the lion's jaws.

The pattern seems to be repeating itself across the iPhone development landscape at the moment. Hardly a day passes without a story of another independent developer with a hit app being bought up by the very corporations under whose control it would have been impossible to build such a game.

"I think the App Store has attracted two groups," says Oliver. "Those that see it as a major commercial opportunity, and those that see it as way to get their creations out there — and obviously in many cases there is a considerable overlap."

WHEN INDIE MEETS CORPORATE

It's strange, perhaps, that a struggle between independent bedroom programmers and corporations should be a hot topic. After all, in almost any other industry, it's good news to find the financial backing of an investor. But the app world is quirky, and has no obvious parallel in any business that has gone before. The App Store represents an unexpected partnership between the homebrew, indie artist and the retail arm of the world's biggest corporation (Apple Inc). Because of this, an emotional component comes into play. People really care about the apps they make, and in many cases their output is arguably "art" and developers are "artists." The conflict between artists and the "aristocracy" — in this modern instance the games multinationals — has raged since the beginning of civilization. The difference today is that the artists have a retail channel — the App Store — powered by the figurehead of capitalist enterprise, Apple Inc. It's the most bizarre fusion of interests that you could imagine. Supercharged capitalism meets indie.

The corporate bodysnatching of the indie iPhone developer scene is a popular business maneuver and it may eventually provoke a full-on intellectual war between the creatives and the corporates. As a realization dawns on small developers that companies like EA can offer little more than an advertising budget, these traditional games publishers could find the indies stop selling out to them. EA, and companies like it, appear to be banking on the fear — and in some cases, the greed — of small developers. The corporate giants are desperately poaching young studios in this brief moment before the indies realize their true worth.

"Making a high-quality app is hard enough, but creating one that is successful presents another set of challenges," cautions Oliver. "I've seen some great games that just haven't been noticed, or that might pop up in the charts briefly, only to be buried by the avalanche of new apps released every day."

> *"Last time I looked at the stats there were over 500 new apps added to the store daily - creating something that stands out and is able to sustain success is not easy."*

It's this "fear of obscurity" among indie developers that makes it so tempting to team up with a traditional games company. But the gamer community tends to react to buy-outs in horror.

"This could be the nail in the coffin for indie devs," wrote a user called *NinthNinja* on the Touch Arcade forums after learning about Firemint's sale to EA. "The more developers [who the big games multinationals] buy up [the more these multinationals] can control the App Store…Once that happens, EA will just produce the games that make money… sequel after sequel of the same game. Just like they do on the console markets."

THE RISKS OF SELLING OUT

It's difficult to reconcile this perspective with that of the industry magazine *TGR* (*The Game Reviews*), which argued in a memorable staff editorial that "Indie Games Will Only Be Successful When They Sell Out."

"Here's a simple reality check when it comes to publishing a game," wrote *TGR*. "In order for indie games to ever have a chance to honestly compete with more mainstream fare, they must be published under the wing of a large company. As much as people hate to admit it, giants like Activision and EA have a lot of clout in determining what games get made, and independent developers would do well to really lean on these companies to create indie wings."

The *TGR* piece illustrates a major problem with the industry line on indie acquisitions: The industry is profoundly confused about what an indie games studio actually is. *TGR* seem oddly unaware of the paradox in suggesting that an independent studio creates "indie wings" by selling out to a company like EA. For such a statement to make sense it would require a redefinition of "indie" so that it means something quite different from "independent." How can a studio be both EA-owned and independent at the same time?

This type of word play is a tactic being played out across the iPhone developer scene. Giant publishing companies are using a semantic trick to make acquisitions more palatable to small studios, twisting the meaning of "indie" to mean something else entirely. Quite what the word means to the giants like EA is unclear, but a loose definition might be "largely unsupervised," or "not hassled too much by us for the moment." But will this be true for the long term?

EAT THE RICH

There are numerous examples of this clever tactic being used by corporate giants to woo indie developers.

The small development house, Smashing Ideas, was recently acquired by Random House. Shortly afterwards, Smashing Ideas' CEO made a statement that, "The beauty of our relationship with Random House is that we will stay an independent company."

Again, the language is revealing. The "acquisition" is reframed as a "relationship" and, despite now being owned by a wing of one of the biggest media conglomerates on the planet, the CEO claims the studio is "independent."

It would be a mistake to put his choice of words down to self-delusion. In fact, it's a very clever use of language prescribed directly by Random House to conceal a reality where larger publishers are swallowing up legions of smaller ones under the guise of "helping" them into a "relationship." What is actually happening is that the dinosaurs of traditional publishing are engaged in a wholesale land-grab of the small-developer scene. Because the indie developer community is filled with artists and dreamers, the corporates are adapting their language to cushion the psychological blow of buy-outs.

The question now is: How will the developer community continue to react to this assault by traditional publishers? These corporate giants were essential in an age where distributing software required manufacturing plants, truck drivers, shipping and brick-and-mortar stores, but now they are at risk of being cut out of the retail chain. What distribution advantage can the traditional publisher offer a developer over the App Store (the world's biggest software retail outlet)?

EXPLOITING A FEAR OF FAILURE

TGR suggests that developers should live in fear of selling games without the marketing support of a company like EA because "making a great game doesn't mean squat if no one knows about it."

But perhaps it is the traditional publishers who should live in fear. Perhaps they should fear that the indie developer may soon realize that paying a regular marketing company to promote an app is far more profitable than selling out to the fretful dinosaurs.

> *"Apple is already the publisher for indie developers," says Mills from ustwo. "Do developers really need two publishers?"*

SUMMARY

Here's a roundup of the important points covered in this chapter:

- Many small, independent iPhone developers have demonstrated that huge amounts of cash can be made from the App Store. But now that a viable market has established itself, larger corporate interests are stepping in to gobble up any indie studio that smells like money.

- The corporate giants fishing for indie app teams face a paradox: The apps they admire could not have been created under the traditional studio system. Independent development on the iPhone has been successful precisely because designers and programmers have been left free to express themselves outside a corporate structure. The irony of the situation is that, in buying up indie developers, many larger games studios are destroying the very environment that gave rise to the success they crave.

- Tensions between the corporations and indie developers are just the latest chapter in a struggle between individual artists and the aristocracy that has run for many hundreds of years. But now the tables have turned. The aristocracy no longer controls the means of production — independent developers are free to manufacture and distribute software through the App Store without the interference of wealthy holders of capital. Traditional publishers can offer very little to the iPhone developer apart from a large cash sum, in exchange for turning over their companies. Afraid for their existence, large software studios must attempt to convince indie developers that they cannot succeed without rapid expansion and an injection of capital. However, the reality is that many Appillionaires are making an extremely good living independently. The traditional software corporations live in fear that this realization will spread across the software industry and that app development will continue to decentralize, leaving the traditional giants struggling to compete on merit against of hundreds of smaller, more agile and creative developers.

12

LIFE IN THE TRENCHES

I'm forever blowing bubbles,

Pretty bubbles in the air.

They fly so high,

Nearly reach the sky,

Then like my dreams,

They fade and die.

I'M VISITING ONE of London's exclusive private members clubs. I've been invited here to meet two recent university graduates who have persuaded their friends and families to invest in an app idea that they think will change the world. We drink by the rooftop pool and they describe their app to me. It begins, as always, with an explanation of why their idea is special, a rare gem that will stand out from the 5 billion other apps on the store. I listen carefully to their plans and they show me a demo of their app. They are not programmers, but one of them is a designer and has created the graphics for the app. They tell me that, so far, development has cost $16,000 and they're not finished yet.

AN EXPENSIVE GAME

Their development cost is typical for a simple app. It's estimated that the average iPhone app costs between $15,000 and $50,000 to produce — not including marketing. For comparison, take an app like *Alice in New York*, the sequel to *Alice for the iPad*. This was a bedroom project with a shoestring budget and it cost around $20,000 to develop — excluding my time. Also consider Atomic Antelope's collaboration with ustwo, *Nursery Rhymes with Storytime*. This was a full studio project, with salaried employees working on the code and artwork. It cost over $60,000 to produce, excluding marketing and my time. Both these projects were relatively simple interactive books. To create a productivity app, or a game, is significantly more expensive. Bedroom programmers can eliminate much of these costs by doing all the coding and design work themselves — the first *Alice* app, for example, cost nothing except time. Increasingly, young entrepreneurs with no program-ming experience are now choosing to employ outside help to build their iPhone app ideas, making the projects extremely expensive. The unfortunate truth of the market is that most of these entrepreneurs will never recoup their investments. Ever.

The most cynical estimate is that the median app makes $682 per year for its developer on the App Store, according to Tomi T. Ahonen, author of the book *Communities Dominate Brands*. If this figure is accurate — and it's hard to be completely certain because Apple do not release detailed data publicly — then half the developers in the App Store may actually be earning less than $682 per year. This figure chimes true for me, since some of Atomic Ante-lope's early apps have made less than this in the year since they were released. If a developer makes money, it tends to be from the rare breakout successes that recoup all the losses it took to get there.

One of the author's apps, *Alice in New York,* cost around $20,000 to create, on a shoestring budget. The author took his salary entirely as a percentage of revenue to save on production costs.

SOURCE: Reproduced with permission of Atomic Antelope © 2011 Atomic Antelope.

PULLING BACK THE CURTAIN

Apple has released some very telling bits of information about the App Store, and Ahonen has used this to draw some intriguing conclusions on the state of the industry. We know, for example, that 5 billion apps were downloaded during the time from when the App Store opened, up until the summer of 2010. We also know that the amount paid out to developers in that time was $980 million. It's estimated that somewhere between 14.7 percent to 18 percent of apps are paid downloads, and from this we can extrapolate the median $682 per year income for an iOS developer.

The interesting thing about these figures is that they provoke a mild outrage in the community when you confront developers with the cold facts. Many online forums are filled with developers who cannot understand why the gold-rush narrative peddled by the mass media is not reflected in the reality of selling software on the App Store. The masses were sold the Appillionaire dream, but the reality was a few hundred dollars in a jam jar — and that's if they're lucky.

"Making a high-quality app is hard enough," says Oliver James, creator of *Rolando*, "but making one that is successful presents another set of challenges. I've seen some great games that just haven't been noticed, or that might pop up in the charts briefly, only to be buried by the avalanche of new apps released every day - creating something that stands out and is able to sustain success is not easy."

It's sometimes difficult to know whether to react with sympathy to the repeated failures on the App Store — I've been there myself — or to simply shrug and dismiss it as the way of the world. While many developers accept defeat with good grace, with others you feel a sense of entitlement that is suffocating. But, for a sobering comparison, you might take a look at the number of scripts submitted to Hollywood every year compared to the number of screenwriters actually making money. Or look at the number of novels submitted to publishers, compared to the number that turn a profit. The truth of the matter is that success in any creative discipline is exceptionally difficult and the bulk of profit tends to come from a tiny niche of super-successful titles. For every *Doodle Jump* or *Cut the Rope* there are several thousand flops. The App Store is littered with dreams of app superstardom that ended in catastrophe, and this is just the beginning.

Back in the private members club with the two graduates. They're explaining to me how their app idea is strong enough to become a break-through hit on the App Store. One of them keeps visiting the bathroom and is clearly on some kind of drug binge — his eyes are magnificent sunsets and at one point he leans in close as if to share a secret.

Rolando, one of the iPhone's best-loved platform games.

SOURCE: Reproduced with permission of Oliver James © 2011 Oliver James.

"Yeah, of course they don't get it," he says. "But we get it. It's show business. You work on this app stuff for months, you've got no idea if it will work or not. Then one day: Swoosh," he throws his hands up in the air. "The stage curtain comes up and either everybody claps and cheers, or they stare at you and walk out. Making apps is like show business. You can rehearse, but it doesn't mean anything. You've got to have the magic."

Although it's a surprisingly accurate description of the app market, there's a concerned look on the other graduate's face. He has a more optimistic view of their app and is confused by his business partner's uncertainty. While his partner ponders the ups and downs of the entertainment industry, he seems convinced that the game they've created will be a massive hit.

TRUST-FUND FANTASIES

The App Store has evolved far beyond its original appeal to just hobbyist programmers and designers. Now the same demographic that Apple woos in its marketing campaigns are looking to apps as an investment opportunity. Remember Apple's famous Mac vs PC ads, the ones where the Mac was played by Justin Long in jeans and a T-shirt and the PC by John Hodgman in a starched suit? It's strange to note that many of the kids now investing their trust funds in app ideas look so much like the Mac guy. Perhaps it was a predictable evolution: if they own an iPod, an iMac, and an iPhone, what more logical step for the wealthy hipster than to get an iJob? "App developer" is fast becoming a trendy off-the-shelf identity for the rich and confused — just as running a website was in the dotcom bubble. The problem is that Apple tends to deliver on its promises: if you buy an iPhone or an iPad, you're likely to be one of the majority of users who are extremely satisfied with their experience. It's then easy to be fooled into thinking that becoming an app developer is also a kind of product, and that you deserve to enjoy it.

Joining up as an app developer looks and feels like every other Apple experience, slickly delivered and well managed, but in the end the developer must contend with the reality of market forces, and in many cases, the cruel hand of fate. An unintended consequence of Apple's prowess at marketing the App Store is that being an iPhone "game developer" has become as much a status symbol to some people as toting a MacBook Pro, but success is elusive.

> As Mills from ustwo puts it, "Commercial suicide backed by other people's money has become the norm in the game industry since the mid 1990s."

The App Store developer sign-up process. It's as slick as buying an iPod but, unlike other Apple products, satisfaction is reliant on your persistence and ingenuity.

SOURCE: Reproduced with permission of Apple Inc © 2011 Apple Inc.

INTO THE MAINSTREAM

In the past year, the App Store has completed its journey out into popular culture, singing a crescendo with the tie-in deal between *Angry Birds* and the animated feature film, *Rio*. It's this mainstream visibility, and the App Store's reputation in the media as a path to fortune and glory, that has attracted a new breed of app developer — one who sees the App Store purely as a financial investment rather than a creative one. Simon Oliver, creator of *Rolando*, recognizes this division.

"I think the App Store has attracted two groups - those who see it as a major commercial opportunity, and those who see it as way to get their creations out there," says Oliver, "and obviously in many cases there is a considerable overlap."

PROGRAMMERS AS SUPERSTARS

Perhaps it was inevitable, when the company behind the marketing success of the iMac and the iPod turned its hand to promoting independent software development, that the public image of developers would change forever. Apple has literally transformed the social acceptability of programmers and overseen the rise of the geek.

As Daniel Wood — owner of indie app studio Runloop — explains it, "Apple has done the seemingly impossible: they've made developing cool. A few years ago the man on the street didn't want software, or talk about software. Now suddenly everyone's like, 'have you seen this app, have you seen that app — it makes your face into a fat person!' People have been trying to do this for ages, make programming cool. They used titles like 'creative developer,' but it basically just means programmer. Somehow Apple did the impossible."

It is this, the cool-ification of programming, that might be the greatest trick Apple has ever pulled. At dinner parties where the job title of programmer was treated with about as much interest as surveyor, now suddenly we have entered an era of programmer as superstar.

PROGRAMMERS AS RIVALS

Just as rock bands have rivalries, so do app developers. But rather than a physical confrontation backstage, the developers use more surreptitious means of attack. Tactics range from writing bad reviews of their rival's apps on iTunes, through to contacting Apple to snitch on their competitor's minor violations of the App Store rules. Then there are the app developers who use shills to post positive reviews of their own apps, to create an impression that an app is far better than it actually is.

Some go even further. Vietnamese iPhone developer Thuat Nguyen had all of his apps pulled from the store by Apple on account of "fraudulent purchase patterns" — it transpired that the reason Nguyen's apps were topping the charts was that he had hacked into iTunes accounts and used stolen credit card numbers to buy his apps into a leading position. More than 40 of the top 50 apps in the Books category were occupied by the developer before Apple pulled the plug.

Then there's the developer-on-developer fighting. Back in February 2009, *Pull My Finger* app developer Air-O-Matic contacted Apple to complain that rival developer, InfoMedia, developer of *iFart Mobile*, was committing an "abuse of our trademark" and "planting negative reviews of the apps of his competitors and positive reviews of his own… disparaging his competition with testimonials."

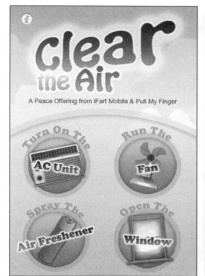

Clear the Air by Air-O-Matic and InfoMedia. Two developers who found themselves embroiled in a copyright dispute. Eventually the companies settled amicably, launching this app together as a gesture of peace.

SOURCE: Reproduced with permission of Air-O-Matic © 2011 Air-O-Matic.

The dispute hinged on both company's use of the phrase "pull my finger," which Air-O-Matic insisted was their trademark right, but which InfoMedia claimed was a "common descriptive phrase" and one they had every right to use.

A bitter dispute followed, with Air-O-Matic's lawyers demanding $50,000 in compensation, first telling InfoMedia, "Your client's actions have cost Air-O-Matic significant sales volume, revenues, and now legal fees to rectify," and then in later correspondence, "Air-O-Matic is not ready to speak directly with your client because it has been financially harmed by InfoMedia's deliberate efforts to bump its app from its leading sales position on Apple though use of unfair trade tactics. *Pull My Finger* fell precipitously from being the #1 iPhone application as a direct result of InfoMedia's systemic efforts to profit from the *Pull My Finger* name and leverage the buzz around it."

Apple refused to intervene, asking the developers to resolve the issue between themselves. The result of the court action was one of the most ridiculous complaint documents you'll ever read, which ultimately led to a settlement between InfoMedia and Air-O-Matic. Unlike many similar confrontations, the rivalry ended amicably with the two companies releasing a free app together called *Clear the Air*.

iBeer by Molson Coors. Hottrix took legal action against Molson Coors when the beverage giant decided to make this clone of Hottrix's best-selling app and give it away for free. Hottrix ultimately won the legal battle.

SOURCE: Reproduced with permission of Hottrix © 2011 Hottrix.

The most famous dispute to date has been between Hottrix, creators of the *iBeer* app, and Molson Coors, the drinks company that launched a very similar free app called *iPint*.

Hottrix's *iBeer* simulates the drinking of a virtual liquid when the iPhone is tilted towards a user's mouth. It is one of the most successful iPhone apps ever created, but also the most heavily litigated. When Coors released a copycat app called *iPint*, Hottrix's lawyers pounced, issuing Coors with a $12.5 million lawsuit on behalf of what Hottrix's attorney described as "a mom-and-pop company who just wants to protect their intellectual property rights."

Steve Sheraton, the programmer behind *iBeer*, was approached by Coors to develop an app like *iBeer* soon after Sheraton's original was launched on the store, but he turned down the offer from the drinks company. In response, Coors began work on their own version of the app, but unlike Sheraton's *iBeer*, Coors version was launched as a free app because it would be used to promote the company's Carling beer. When the rival app appeared on the store, Sheraton was outraged.

"As *iPint* increased in popularity, *iBeer* decreased in popularity," stated the lawsuit, "since end users could get ostensibly the same application without a direct cost (besides viewing the Carling advertising) of paying $2.99 for *iBeer*."

Apple eventually pulled Coors' *iPint* app from the store, causing *iBeer* to rise back up through the charts again, but it wasn't the end for Hottrix's legal wrangles.

Things got even more peculiar for Sheraton when the confectionary giant Hershey's launched a copycat app to rival Hottrix's own *iMilk* app. The Hershey's app was a similar design to *iBeer*, but used milk instead of beer. The only problem was: Hottrix was already selling this app and had been for almost two years. All the more surprising was the fact that Sheraton had been emailed by Hershey's asking him to develop the app. When Sheraton refused, the company went ahead without him.

"We invent *iMilk* in 2007; make it an iTunes best-seller in 2008," said Sheraton, "Hershey's emails us and wants it, then releases an unauthorized, infringing copy in 2009. We call Hershey's on it; they run to the judge and sue us… Considering our *iMilk* has been around for three years and Hershey's 'own' *iMilk* iPhone app only just showed up recently, after they wanted it programmed by us, we're unimpressed."

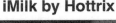

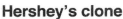

Hottrix's *iMilk* was shamelessly cloned by Hershey's. The companies then threw themselves into a legal battle.

SOURCE: Reproduced with permission of Hottrix © 2011 Hottrix.

Sheraton soon launched a $12 million counterclaim against Hershey's, to which the chocolate company responded, "Unlike the Hottrix application, the Hershey's Chocolate Milk iPhone application 'milk' cannot be 'drunk' from the iPhone by tipping the phone (which is the only mechanism for drinking the milk in the Hottrix application), but can only be 'drunk' by use of the virtual straw."

THE COST OF WAR

Sheraton was in a financial position to defend his company from the multinationals swooping in to crush his apps, but many others have not been so lucky. The App Store is awash with knock-offs of rival apps — and whether you are an advocate of intellectual property rights for software or not — many developers find something slightly insidious about the corporations that have stepped in to capitalize on the creative ideals of the indie scene.

FEEDING TIME

The *iBeer* fiasco is just the tip of the iceberg for corporate interest in the app scene. The traditional software publishers are currently engaged in a land grab across the app development scene — a land grab that does little to dispel the mythology surrounding the Appillionaires. If you thought the

Appillionaires were making a lot of money on the App Store, consider what they can make by selling out. Barely a week goes by without a giant media conglomerate reaching out a slimy proboscis and suckering up another independent app developer. The sums of money involved get more and more spectacular with every twist and turn of the app story. Whether it's Electronic Arts snapping up *Angry Birds'* creator Chillingo ($20 million in cash — although the deal excluded EA from any cut for *Angry Birds* and *Cut the Rope*) and *Flight Control* developers' Firemint ($20-40 million), or social games goliath Zynga buying Wonderland Software, it looks increasingly difficult for an app developer to operate successfully and still resist the incredible sums available if they sell.

Electronic Art's Barry Cottle, vice president and general manager of EA Interactive, justified the company's acquisition of Firemint.

"As the handset market has got more fragmented, so has the developer space," Cottle explained. "There's a plethora of really talented small shops out there able to get a breakthrough hit that people believe is repeatable. So this notion of small developers being acquired by larger players is probably more the type of acquisition that you're going to see going forward."

THE BIG MONEY

Cottle is wrong about the fragmentation of the handset market. For profitable apps at least, the market is *less* fragmented than ever — for better or worse, the App Store currently stands alone as a viable outlet for indie developer projects. Total iPhone developer income in 2010 was $1.7 billion while for Android developers it was just $103 million. It's also estimated that 71 percent of mobile app downloads were to iOS devices and only 5 percent to Android. A report by *IHS Screen Digest* projects that Apple will make $2.91 billion from apps in 2011, and Android the comparatively smaller figure of $425 million.

The fragmentation Cottle describes is hard to locate. However, he's right about one thing, the "larger players" are definitely out on the prowl for successful independents. The question is: Can these independents stay nimble while simultaneously tied by reins to these vast toppling media giants of the past?

A CERTAIN NAIVETÉ

The naivety of these multinational publishers can often exceed even that of hipsters wielding their trust funds. Rupert Murdoch's purchase of MySpace back in July 2005 for US$580 million is often wheeled out as the best example of this corporate mindlessness — MySpace was recently sold for an estimated $35 million — one in a recent spate of huge embarrassments for Murdoch. An age-old theme persists: the CEO's grand idea that to embody the values of a group of a team you admire, you simply have to buy them and all the "greatness" will rub off. The problem is, when you have that much money, who is going to say no? Or, as Warren Buffett put it, "Of one thing be certain: if a CEO is enthused about a particularly foolish acquisition, both his internal staff and his outside advisors will come up with whatever projections are needed to justify his stance. Only in fairy tales are emperors told that they are naked."

For the few corporations that have been successful in entering the App Store, the result has often been a giant shift in market for all developers.

A WICKED GAME

In December, all iOS developers compete for a place in the top ten, a crucial position for the holiday season. Apple freezes the rankings for a few days over Christmas, so this time of year is critical for developers. Whatever chart position an app finds itself in before the freeze, it will stay there over the entire Christmas period — an incredible boon for the lucky few apps that are ranked in top positions when this freeze begins. When hundreds of thousands of people power-up their new iPhones or iPads on Christmas day, these top-ranked apps are the first the customer will see in the store, and are the apps they are most likely to buy.

In December 2010, something unusually aggressive happened. The gaming giant Electronic Arts (EA) suddenly slashed the prices of over 70 of its games to 99 cents, intensifying a price drop across all gaming apps for the holiday season. The pressure on competing developers to make similar price drops was enormous and many followed EA's lead.

The Christmas app frenzy is a once-yearly event but it's a microcosm of the problem now facing developers all year round: a race to the bottom on prices. If it wasn't hard enough for developers to make their app a success on the store, the business gets all the more cutthroat when consumers have begun to expect so much functionality from a 99-cent app, especially in the games category. British writer, Charlie Brooker, has led a charge against the public's extraordinarily high expectations of what a cheap app can deliver. After reading a string of negative reviews on the App Store that demonstrated that public's "languid sense of entitlement," he was drawn to pen an article on the subject.

"Look at the App Store. Read the reviews of novelty games costing [99 cents]," Brooker wrote in *The Guardian*. "Lots of slaggings — which is fair enough when you're actively warning other users not to bother shelling out for something substandard. But they often don't stop there. In some cases, people insist the developers should be jailed for fraud, just because there weren't enough levels for their liking. I once read an absolutely scathing one-star review in which the author bitterly complained that a game had only kept him entertained for four hours."

"FOUR HOURS? FOR [99 cents]? AND YOU'RE ANGRY ENOUGH TO WRITE AN ESSAY ABOUT IT? ON YOUR EXPENSIVE IPHONE? HAVE YOU LOST YOUR MIND?"

As Brooker points out, public expectations have reached an all-time high. But, at such a low price, the individual developer, or app studio, must make up the cost of building the app through an extremely high volume of sales at these low price points. The problem is, there is room at the top of the charts for only a finite number of apps that can return this volume of sales.

The majority of consumers buy apps based on the promotional banners Apple runs on iTunes, or by scanning the top-ten list. If an app is not visible in either of these places, it's very hard for the developer to generate any sales.

Visibility has always been a problem in the App Store, and Apple has worked to fix it. Originally, the top-100 ranks were based exclusively on an app's unit sales, not its revenue. This meant that lower-priced apps could take advantage of the system, riding high on unit sales, while more expensive apps — which may have been making more money — were pushed down the charts. Because unit sales were the only metric the App Store charts were using, many developers argued that Apple was encouraging a 99-cent economy and, by doing so, actively discouraging heavy investment in more expensive, and more capable, apps. In response to the outcry, Apple introduced a new chart that displayed the "Top Grossing" apps in every category, as well as across the entire App Store. But it was too late.

PRICES ARE LOW

Within just a few months of the iPhone's launch, the 99-cent price became set in the consumer's mind as the default cost of an iPhone app and developers have struggled with this expectation ever since. The resentment of the indie developer community is best expressed by development studio ustwo, which began a campaign to save the App Store from becoming a ghetto of 99-cent apps. The company proudly announced on its website "F**k 99 cents. I'd rather charge nothing than that insult price."

Mills from ustwo, the self-styled "Willy Wonka of Apps," is the industry's most eccentric and outspoken developer.

SOURCE: Reproduced with permission of Thomas Farnetti © 2011 Thomas Farnetti.

Ustwo co-founder, Mills, explained, "The problem is for us it's currently a false economy. There may have been 2 billion app downloads and counting so far, but we cannot ignore the fact that most indie developers out there are making absolutely nothing — in fact most are losing money."

"The emergence of the 99-cent price point 100 percent kick-started the app store phenomenon as we know it today, but the bottom line is that it's impossible to make money at the 99-cent price point for 99 percent of studios. I'm talking about enough money to actually allow you to survive on app sales alone. If people are not making money then clearly there is no market, just the illusion of one created by the hope of hitting the jackpot."

EXPECTATIONS ARE HIGH

What is at the heart of the 99-cent puzzle? Why are consumers so brutally demanding when it comes to 99-cent apps? The same people who have splashed out many hundreds of dollars on one of the most expensive phones on the market will regularly write horrible, damning reviews of 99-cent software that fails to meet their expectations. But, given that these apps cost less than a can of soda, why are expectations so high?

Developer Ian Bogot attempted to rationalize this behavior in a piece entitled "Persuasive Games: I Want My 99¢ Back," in which he voiced the fury of many indie iPhone developers.

The 99-Cent Buyer Is a Different Animal

The high expectations laid on the 99-cent app is a phenomena I've witnessed as a developer myself. One popular book app we launched was initially priced at $3.99. It received glowing reviews from hundreds of customers. Then, in an effort to increase sales, we lowered the price to 99 cents. The effect was instant. Suddenly terrible reviews started pouring in; the extent of the hatred was overwhelming. Many people did not feel the app was worth 99 cents and demanded refunds.

Reeling from the shock, we raised the price to $1.99 and all the negative reviews stopped, and most mysteriously of all, the app continued to make as much money as it had at 99 cents. The revenue remained steady, but the bad reviews were nowhere to be seen. The book market is different from the games market on the App Store, but the experiment demonstrated something quite revealing for all app categories: The consumers who buy apps at 99 cents are clearly motivated by a psychological mechanism that is very different from the one motivating those who buy above this price.

"When we buy something for a very low price, we are conditioned to see it as expendable," wrote Bogot. "What costs a dollar these days? Hardly anything. A cup of coffee. A pack of sticky notes. A Jr. Bacon Cheeseburger. A lottery ticket. Stuff we use up and discard… I contend that iPhone players are not so much dissatisfied as they are confused. Should one treat a 99-cent game as a piece of ephemera, or as a potentially rich experience?"

Nursery Rhymes with Storytime. The author was part of the team working on this app. When priced at 99 cents, the app was flooded with bad reviews. When the price was raised to $3.99, the reviews became more positive. Bizarrely, the audience buying at $3.99 was more receptive to the app.

SOURCE: Reproduced with permission of Atomic Antelope and ustwo
© 2011 Atomic Antelope and ustwo.

"Apparently 99 cents is a risk worth taking on a cup of coffee," laments Bogot, "but not on a sophisticated, long-form videogame worth ten times more on another platform." It's a conclusion that many other developers have made, like Dan Grigsby.

"Lower your price, lower your ratings," says Grigsby. "Lower ratings, lower social proof. Lower social proof, lower sales. That's my theory." Grigsby points to developer Pete Schwamb, who witnessed a huge ratings decline for his app *Cricket Song* when he dropped the price.

Schwamb describes the users who purchased at this lower cost as "uninvested." He believes that consumers who spent more than 99 cents on an app feel a psychological pressure to believe that their purchases are worthwhile. As a bizarre result, these users will tend emphasize their positive feelings to justify their decisions, hence: better reviews.

This does explain why more expensive apps tend to be ranked more positively — if we ignore other factors, like the quality of the app. But it doesn't fully explain the collective race to 99 cents, nor does it explain why users are quite so profoundly embittered by a 99-cent app that they are relatively happy with at $1.99.

In April 2011, Mike Capps, CEO of Epic Games — who make the *Gears of War* franchise — told Industry Gamers that 99-cent games would be the death of the industry. Capps was worried that the industry might not be sustainable if games gravitate toward the iPhone model.

"We have not been this uncertain about what's coming next in the games industry since Epic's been around for 20 years," explained Capps. "We're at such an inflection point. Will there be physical distribution in 10 years or even five? Will anyone care about the next console generation? If there's anything that's killing us, it's dollar apps. How do you sell someone a $60 game that's really worth it?"

There's no mistaking that apps are getting cheaper and cheaper, making an already precarious marketplace all the more risky for developers looking to turn a profit. But there is an alternative argument for the rise of the 99-cent app, although companies like Epic don't want to hear it.

WHO REALLY BENEFITS FROM 99-CENT GAMES?

The unspoken reason so many iPhone apps can be priced at 99 cents is that they didn't cost much money to make, they just cost time. They were built by small teams, often one or two people, working in their spare hours, hoping for a breakout hit. The 99-cent price is unsustainable for Epic, or EA, and even medium-sized development studios like ustwo, but it is not unsustainable for the legions of dreamers in their bedrooms.

As one forum member on #AltDevBlogADay puts it, "The other way of looking at it is that the 99-cent price point is our indie market, and the big boys are muscling in and stealing it. If they can't sell at premium prices, they become indie bullies."

This counterargument runs that big software companies like Epic are tactically undercutting the bedroom programmers by taking a loss on the majority of their titles until the point that the indie programmer is forced down the charts, out of sight. The main reason a 99-cent economy currently exists is that the bedroom programmers created it. It's not necessarily a viable model for the bigger companies in the App Store game, but they'll play along until the indie developer is forced out of competition. Not everyone is surprised at the elaborate game being played out on the iOS platform.

"We can't get rich sitting at home and making our indie game?" asks developer James Podesta, feigning horror. "That only became a problem when suddenly, for the first time ever, we could get rich sitting at home and making an indie game. This is not the norm and may not stay that way as people with more money behind them do what they always do and find good ways to use their money to make more money."

Podesta — who has developed games for studios like Codemasters — believes there are two major forces battling it out on the App Store. The first group is the established games companies who invest large amounts of money into titles for which they will eventually charge between $5 and $10. These traditional companies are currently in competition with the "garage indies" who make "low-content games" priced between 99 cents and $1.99 in the hope that their app might "go viral" and make them an Appillionaire.

"Indies are reduced to a lottery system," says Podesta. "Which is more than we ever had before, although the gold mines at the release of iPhone and then again at the release of iPad are still fresh in memory, making people think its easier than it should be".

A SPECIAL TIME IN HISTORY

A big question mark hangs over how indie developers will compete against the likes of Electronic Arts when both are pricing titles at 99 cents.

"I think it's going to change rapidly over the next couple of years," says Peter Pashley — sole creator of zombie-shooter game *Aftermath*. "There's been a window for the last few years where someone like me can do really well. It's a situation which hasn't existed for the last 15 years."

Aftermath, created by developer Peter Pashley. The game looks like a major studio title, but was built by just one man, working alone.

SOURCE: Reproduced with permission of Peter Pashley © 2011 Peter Pashley.

"But I think there will be a point technologically where a single person won't be able to take advantage of all the power the hardware has to offer. I imagine that because there's this race to the bottom on price point, some teams are never going to be able to compete at that price point."

"But," he adds hopefully, "people working alone that are multitalented, don't need big teams. So there's always a chance for success at that lower price point."

Simon Oliver — creator of *Rolando* — is not so optimistic.

"As with the majority of media coverage, only the most extreme stories will get picked up," says Oliver. "It's sometimes made to appear that the App Store is a place of limitless opportunity and guaranteed success, which has definitely contributed to the gold-rush effect. The stories of the thousands of developers who have created Apps that have failed to take off or have lost a considerable amount of money are never reported."

In the winter of 2010, a few voices began to question the Appillionaire mythology. "Is the App Gold Rush Already Over?" asked industry pundit Doug Dyer, who went on to draw a direct parallel to the historical events of the California gold rush in the 19th century and the modern day Appillionaire story.

"Is developing apps the latest version of the Gold Rush?" pondered Dyer. "As I recall from elementary school history, when the world's masses flooded to Sutter's Mill and the Klondike, very few ever actually found anything of value."

Dyer resisted the temptation to push the metaphor any further, given that nobody was actually dying in the pursuit of App Store fame, but he wrote that "we're past the land-grab stage of the app," and eventually concluded that in fact the App Store gold rush was in fact not over, "Not by a long shot."

A few months later, Peter Molyneux — a developer at Lionhead studios — recognized the problems that would face the first wave of Appillionaires at the market matured.

"It's inevitable that a *Star Wars* or Disney game, a five million dollar iPhone project, will be released." Molyneux told *Industry Gamer*. "And when it does, consumers are going to like it. They're going to say 'I can pay 99 cents for this [indie iPhone game] or I can pay 99 cents for this [triple-A iPhone game]."

One problem is that the end of the gold rush has been called so many times, by so many different people, that it's difficult for anyone to be certain if it really has ended, and how much power the bedroom developer still wields.

The corporations edging in on the App Store would certainly like it to be true that the indie developer faces a decline in fortune, but they overlook one very important thing: the uniquely egalitarian distribution mechanism for apps.

Traditional games companies and media conglomerates are used to a system where they control the means by which a product is manufactured and delivered. For example, Disney does not compete with indie filmmakers selling tickets for competing films in the same cinema. Disney controls the production and distribution of its films because, to some extent, it controls the cinemas. But in the new model, the App Store model, no company is on higher footing than any other in the distribution channel. No company can block another company's efforts and apps must, to some degree, compete on an intellectual level with other apps. It's as close to a capitalist utopia for retail as we may ever see in the software world. Some developers believe that it may be impossible for the corporate giants to crush the Appillionaires.

"This is a special time in history for programmers," says Marco Mazzoli — creator of *Spirit* — "and I personally think that any dev that doesn't give it a shot now is missing out on a great opportunity. The most wonderful thing about the App Store, is that, most of the time, it's a meritocracy."

> *"Like every other highly competitive marketplace out there, it's not always fair, but generally speaking, the apps with the most love and thought put in them will find their way into the hands of more customers."*

It's this "love and thought" that remains the Appillionaires secret weapon. Passion is the indie programmers' last defense against the corporate giants. The traditional publishing giants, for all their marketing muscle and multi-million dollar cash reserves, often lack key ingredients: creativity and a genuine hunger for success. In swallowing up the indie heroes of the app explosion, like some kind of greedy *Pac-Man* gobbling power-up pills, the corporations now risk destroying the creative spirit that has dominated the early years of the iPhone. It remains to be seen whether a game like *Tiny Wings* or *Doodle Jump* can be created by a corporate giant. It may well turn out that the stifling mechanisms of order, caution, and restraint that keep a multinational functioning will mean the indie developer continues to triumph.

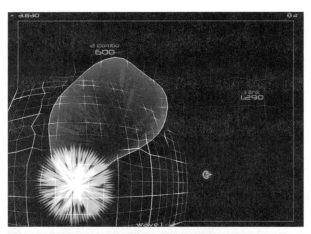

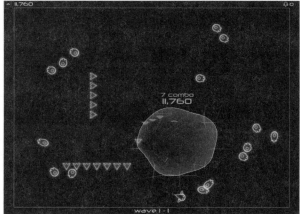

Spirit, created by developer Marco Mazzoli. This hugely successful title demonstrates how creative and productive a solo developer can be when working outside of the major studios.

SOURCE: Reproduced with permission of Marco Mazzoli © 2011 Marco Mazzoli.

The best art is often created when the artist needs no justification for her creations. But the corporate app studios demand justification at every step. The independent developer, however, answers only to himself and can simply begin. Regardless of how much money companies like EA throw at the app scene, the creative advantage may still remain with the Appillionaires.

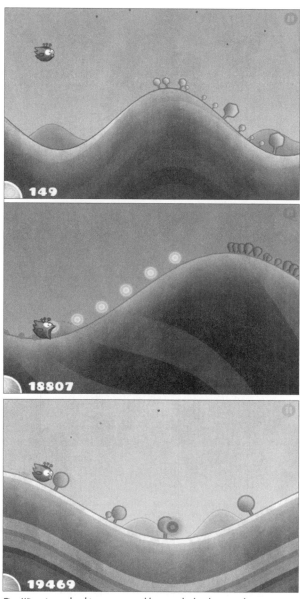

Tiny Wings is another hit game created by a single developer working on an independent project. All the most innovative iPhone games seem to come from programmers working for themselves.

SOURCE: Reproduced with permission of Andreas Illiger © 2011 Andreas Illiger.

THE PATENT THREAT

Although indie iPhone developers have the agility to create new software at a speed wholly foreign to large corporations, they now face a new threat: The patent troll. Whereas larger companies have the cash reserves to combat litigation, the lone iPhone developer struggles to defend themselves when faced with claims of patent violation. At the heart of the problem is a troubling fact: Few developers can know for sure if they are violating a patent until it's too late. And even if they are not violating a patent, the expense of proving this is so enormous that most indie developers would be financially ruined before the case came to court. In addition, there's a bigger problem: Software patents in the United States have been granted so freely, and so widely, that a programmer can hardly write a line of code without being in violation of someone's patent, somewhere.

The industry relies largely on the assumption that few of the available patents will actually be enforced. The U.S. patent system has become so vast and uncharted that some iPhone developers are now choosing to abandon the U.S. market entirely, rather than risk getting hopelessly jammed in the sticky web of patents. Successful iPhone developers like Simon Maddox have quit the U.S. market entirely. Maddox told *The Guardian* he was withdrawing his apps from the U.S. App Store because it was "far too dangerous to do business" there. Craig Hockenberry, who created *Twitterrific*, tweeted, "I became an independent developer to control my own destiny. I no longer do."

Hockenberry has written an article on the subject of patent trolls (those companies that buy software patents specifically for the purpose of extorting money) titled "The Rise and Fall of the Independent Developer," in which he says "it's entirely possible that all the revenue for a product can be eaten up by legal fees. After years of pouring your heart and soul into that product, it's devastating. It makes you question why the hell you're in the business: When you can't pay salaries from product sales, there's no point in building it in the first place. Over the years many of the top-selling apps have been created by independent developers, starting with Steve Demeter and *Trism* at the App Store launch, and continuing to this day with titles like *Tiny Wings* by Andreas Illiger. Losing that kind of talent and innovation to a legal system is the real crime."

Because of the patent threat, a growing movement away from the U.S. App Store has begun, largely provoked by the actions of Lodsys, a company formed with the express purpose of cashing in on a patent for "in-app purchases," which is the system that allows you to buy services from inside an existing app. Lodsys, like many other patent-holding companies, generates no product and provides no service. The company of lawyers exists only to buy old existing patents, discover companies violating these patents, and then demand money from them. Lodsys, and many other companies like it, patrol the world of software developers, looking out for successful businesses to insert their cash-hungry proboscis into.

Thousands of iPhone developers are alleged to be in violation of the Lodsys patent, and many of them are lone programmers, based out of bedrooms across the world. Apple was pushed to intervene, writing to Lodsys:

"Apple requests that Lodsys immediately withdraw all notice letters sent to Apple App Makers and cease its false assertions that the App Makers' use of licensed Apple products and services in any way constitute infringement of any Lodsys patent."

Yet the legal action against small iPhone developers has continued.

It's unknown how the Lodsys saga will play out. But these patents are traded between law firms in a practice that seems so deeply contrary to the U.S. free-market ideology, not to mention basic ethics, that it's difficult to imagine how the patent office can continue to issue and permit the enforcement of software patents without the market grinding to a juddering halt under the weight of suit and countersuit. Patent holders now claim to own the ideas behind mechanisms as obvious as Twitter. A patent-holding company called Kootol claimed that Twitter and a number of iPhone developers had infringed a patent for an "invention [that] allows the user to publish and send messages using one way or two way messaging and by subscribing to posts of other users of a network."

Despite the peculiar fact that many of these patents seem to cover impossibly broad areas of software design, this is sadly no defense for the smaller developer. A developer's innocence is irrelevant and until the system is reformed, many will collapse under the weight of litigation.

SUMMARY

Here's a roundup of the important points covered in this chapter:

- Even a small app can cost many thousands of dollars to develop. With costs averaging between $15,000 to $50,000 for relatively simple apps, unless you're a programmer yourself, expenses can add up very quickly.

- It's estimated that the average app may be earning less than $682 per year. It's hard to decipher the exact figures, but building an app is an extremely risky business. The rewards, however, are potentially huge for the lucky few.

- Somehow Apple has managed the impossible. The company has made programmers cool. No longer are developers at the bottom of the social food chain — it's now considered very stylish to announce that you are an iPhone programmer at a dinner party.

- Oddly, more people are likely to complain about your app if it's priced at 99 cents than if it's priced higher. The worst reviews come from the casual-gaming masses, and they are most likely to buy your app if you price it at 99 cents. Raise the price, and it's very likely you'll get better reviews. Of course, if your app is unusually brilliant, or inherently terrible, it might not matter much either way.

- Corporate giants are muscling in on the app scene, but at a common 99-cent price point, it's unknown whether they can devote considerable resources to the iPhone yet. The risk is too high. For the moment, at least, we are in a golden era for small indie developers to make a fortune.

- Patent "trolls" have begun an apocalypse of litigation against indie iPhone developers. It's a problem that is provoking some developers to quit the U.S. App Store completely. The U.S. software patent system is in desperate need of reform, but while huge corporate interests support its existence, it's a rough ride ahead for some smaller developers.

13

THE FUTURE OF
THE APP

SMARTPHONES — THOSE CELL phones capable of running apps —
now account for well over half of U.S. mobile phone sales and growing. By
2015, it's estimated that the app market will be worth over $37 billion. This
industry-wide change of direction means we're already witnessing a brutal,
turbulent transition from old to new. Many companies that previously
dominated the cell phone market are near collapse. It's a bright, terrifying
new landscape. A place where iconic mobile corporation, Nokia, has
witnessed its profit margins dwindle to nothing, abandoned its core operating system, and watched itself slowly subsumed under the skin of Microsoft,
like a goat being lazily gobbled down by a Burmese python. Across the
mobile industry, former megaliths are toppling, struggling, or being eaten up.

Even early pioneer RIM — the once seemingly unstoppable maker of the
Blackberry phone — has become tragically lost. RIM's management is, at
the time of writing, paddling listlessly as the company's stock price
plummets and its employees write open letters to BGR (Boy Genius
Report) in outright desperation. One employee expressed the hopelessness
at the heart of the company, "I have lost confidence. While I hide it at
work, my passion has been sapped. I know I am not alone — the sentiment
is widespread… If we create great tools, we will see great work. Offer crap
tools and we shouldn't be surprised when we see crap apps. The truth is, no
one in RIM dares to tell management how bad our tools still are. Even our
closest dev partners do their best to say it politely."

THE CHANGING OF THE GUARD

RIM's problem demonstrates the importance of great apps for cell phone sales. Slowly a realization is dawning across the market: Hardware does not sell smartphones. Apps sell smartphones. This is a special moment in computing history. A moment where commodity hardware has largely reached a point where it can — in terms of raw processing power — easily meet the needs of the general consumer. Very slowly, spec-sheet fetishism is dying out. The overwhelming majority of consumers no longer care if their phone has 6MB or 12MB of memory — in fact Apple and others have begun to exclude such information from product spec sheets. The bulk of consumers now expect their smartphone to run quickly and smoothly, like an appliance — it goes without saying. Instead of numbers on a spec sheet, the key differentiator for today's mobile phone buyer is the software on their phones. Apps are king.

Devices that were once useful only for making a phone call to a friend are now packed with every conceivable trick. Today the small box of electronics in our pockets can morph — at the touch of a button — from a simple telephone into a satnav system, mp3 player, video screen, or a credit card replacement. With this rapid acceleration in technology, those companies that have been slower to adapt are quickly running out of oxygen, while others, like Apple and Google, are flourishing.

At the moment, the problem for the industry at wide is that Apple has most of the apps — both in raw numbers and quality of product — and Apple is currently the only company that has demonstrated a solid sales outlet for app developers. Even Rovio, developers of *Angry Birds*, were forced to launch a free ad-supported app on Google's Android because of users' resistance to pay for apps on that platform (it went on to become profitable based on that model, but not all developers have a popular brand to rely on). Far from being an established market, the world of apps could hardly be more interesting and unpredictable, and yet the vast majority of it has yet to be monetized. From the perspective of an indie programmer, the market is risky, but the rewards spectacular. If you thought *Angry Birds* or *Doodle Jump* made a lot of money, you'll be amazed by what bedroom programmers achieve in the next few years.

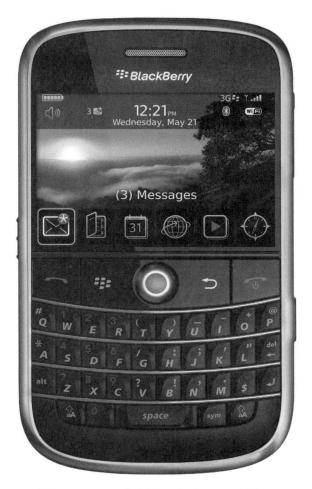

RIM's BlackBerry phone originally led the market but, in a world where consumers expect apps, the company is now struggling to survive.

SOURCE: Reproduced with permission of RIM © 2011 RIM.

WHAT MAKES A KILLER APP?

So, if you wanted to create the next killer app, what could you do to increase your chances of success?

The future of the app — the successful app — relies on the continued ingenuity of the bedroom programmer and the marketing muscle of larger companies. But as the market for apps begins to generate billions of dollars, designers may also begin to look towards the increasingly sophisticated application of behavioral science and biological feedback monitoring. Psychologists are going to have a field day with the app.

There is already something psychologically entrancing about the iPhone and its discrete representation of apps. It has a pleasing alignment of those brightly colored icons, set in a grid pattern like a trophy cabinet of consumer-capitalist candies. From the moment the iPhone is switched on, it appeals to the comfort we feel in symmetry and the simple act of collecting. The hunter-gatherer has ceased to patrol the savannah, and must get his kicks instead from the accumulation of digital "kill," downloaded at 99 cents a time and hoarded on the glossy box in his pocket. We should have little doubt that Apple has considered the psychology of this very primal, human perspective. After all, this is the same company that designed the sleep LED on their MacBook computers to pulse exactly in rhythm with the human respiratory rate when the body is in a state of relaxation. We may wear clothes and chatter in languages, but Apple knows that we remain animals at heart, and pays attention to these details.

THIS IS YOUR BRAIN ON APPS

The psychology of apps is a largely unexplored subject — the App Store hasn't been around long enough for any detailed academic studies on what makes us buy and use apps. There is, however, a wealth of research into videogame psychology and the reward mechanisms present in software-based entertainment. These are likely to hold true in the world of iPhone and iPad software. One of the more interesting studies in this field suggests that although we appear, superficially, to be stimulated by complex challenges and the risk vs reward structure of a game, we do in fact respond very positively to crude graphical events — regardless of whether these graphical events signal a positive or negative software behavior. Far from the post-enlightenment kings and queens of civilization we believe ourselves to be, it turns out that we still get quite a physiological thrill from flashing lights, an exciting noise, and bright colors. A 2005 study by M.I.N.D. Lab/CKIR at the Helsinki School of Economics monitored the facial EMG responses of people playing the videogame *Monkey Bowling 2* and discovered that humans experience a sensation of joy when confronted with a visually exciting event in a game, even if that event has killed their character in the game:

"Unexpectedly, we found that Event 1 (the monkey falls off the edge of the lane to the depth of outer space) elicited an increase in positive affect… Thus, although the event in question represents a clear failure, several physiological indices showed that it elicited positively valences high-arousal emotion (i.e., joy), rather than disappointment. This is an important finding suggesting that event characteristics such as visual impressiveness and exciting-ness may be more potent determinants of the emotional response of the player compared to the meaning of the event in terms of failure or success."

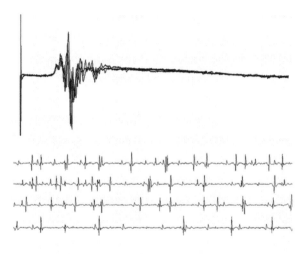

An EMG device can be used by psychologists to measure emotional reactions on the faces of videogame players.

The paper goes on to suggest that facial EMG monitoring could be used to assess the appeal of future games, although it makes the significant point that different personality types displayed different reactions to games depending on whether they were "high impulsive sensation seeking" or "low impulsive sensation seeking" characteristics. Interestingly, this is exactly the same terminology the tobacco industry uses to characterize the audience for their product, along with many other large corporations who evaluate customers on the "sensation seeking scale."

"High impulsive attention seekers" are clinically characterized as having "the tendency to be willing to take risks for the sake of having novel, varied, and intense experiences" according the psychologist Zuckerman. One interesting hypothesis that springs from this categorization system is that the nature of the way the iPhone is used — often in spare moments during the day, a snatched 10-minute break on the train, or between business meetings — means that the behavior of the user is altered so that the bulk of users now fall into the camp of high impulsive sensation seekers for the duration of their experience with the device. This would certainly explain the low attention, low cost and accessible gameplay found in the most popular apps. In an age when the next app experience is only the tap of a finger and 99 cents away, it's little wonder that we are all becoming more impulsive and demanding when we download from the App Store. If you want to build a hit app, and you're not prepared to rely purely on instinct and artistic intuition, you could probably do worse than hook some volunteers up to a facial EMG system and make them play variously tweaked iterations of your software design until they light up the board.

A STRANGE, NEW RELATIONSHIP

It's a *Clockwork Orange* future out there for the app. But, for now at least, there's a glorious and fulfilling opportunity for the individual designer craftsperson to sell their art and ideas through the retail arm of the world's biggest corporation. It's akin to the 18th century blacksmith having his tiny collection of handmade horseshoes personally promoted by the Queen of England around the world; a bizarre collaboration between the smallest craft shop and the biggest commercial entity on the planet.

Apple's relationship with developers is one that would have been socioculturally and logistically impossible in any previous age. What would the industrialists of the 19th century have thought of this empowerment of the individual worker to sell mass-produced goods directly to the customer? And what would Marx have made of Apple's peculiar subversion of the capitalist system with the App Store. He once wrote, "at the core of the capitalist system ... lies the complete separation of the producer from the means of production." But now the producers can build and distribute to millions from their bedrooms.

Of course the App Store system exists within the confines of a complex — and much less honorable — infrastructure of global socioeconomics where vast imbalances of wealth continue to exist. The App Store is clearly not open to those who cannot afford the skills and equipment required. But it still represents a fascinating vision for the future of retail.

For all its faults and detractors, the App Store, and the Appillionaires, may be nothing short of capitalism's most impressive and honorable creative alliance. History has, for a moment, and for a lucky few, come full circle. The small have become big, mainly on the intellectual strength of their ideas and persistence. The App Store represents the beginning of a new and growing software economy where success is awarded on creative merit and smart thinking. An eager audience of millions is now just a mouse-click away.

SUMMARY

Here's a roundup of the important points covered in this chapter:

- The cell phone industry is in a stage of massive upheaval. Established companies are collapsing and traditional software studios are bewildered at the success of indie apps. At the same time, independent developers are pushing the boundaries of software design, selling their creations in a global marketplace via Apple and Google.

- The future of app design may lie in using empirical tests to monitor users as they interact with designs. Using EMG monitors and other devices, it's possible for psychologists to observe physical cues that indicate the emotional state of those interacting with an iPhone app.

- It remains to be seen whether the rise of the Appillionaire will be remembered as a brief, bright spark at the beginning of the 21st century, or if it represents a sea change in the way that software is built and sold. The next decade may, for the software industry, represent a triumph of intellectual talent over the muscle of raw capital. The App Store is a weird new meritocracy where gifted kids in their bedrooms can outsmart the world's richest corporations, using the retail arm of the world's largest corporation as their distribution mechanism. The Appillionaires, and the business model they successfully demonstrate, offer a new hope of creative independence to millions of artists, designers, and programmers across the world.

- If you have a great idea for an app, consider the risks, read the Appillionaires' stories, and roll the dice. The first step is coming up with a great idea; the second is having the persistence to deliver it well. The third component is, of course, the trickiest: Good old-fashioned luck.

Index